THOMAS MANN

THE DEVIL'S ADVOCATE

T. E. APTER

D1515948

New York · New York University Press · 1979

Printed in Great Britain

Acknowledgements

The author and publishers are grateful to Martin Secker & Warburg Ltd and Alfred A. Knopf Inc for permission to reproduce extracts from the English editions of Mann's works.

We are also grateful to Lawrence Pollinger Ltd, the estate of the late Mrs Frieda Lawrence and the Viking Press for permission to quote the extracts from *Women in Love* and *Phoenix* by D. H. Lawrence.

Contents

1 Introduction

Thomas Mann tried to state every claim in the devil's favour. He hoped, with a would-be humanism, that an investigation of evil's force and fascination would result in refreshing disgust with evil, that evil, once exposed, would shrivel in sunlight and crumble in the hands of the clear-eyed. This hope, however, is the point against which his novels, stories and essays move. As he boldly underlines the sometimes grotesque, sometimes elegant course the dæmonic and decadent take, the dark river of corruption fails to reveal an unqualified ugliness; unflaggingly it glows with an hypnotic iridescence and flows with a silky vitality that promises rich and good things.

Mann had to face the crisis of morality, the transformation of values he found in the works of Schopenhauer, Nietzsche and Freud. A person could no longer be seen as governed primarily by consciousness, nor could human impulses be supposed to be educable and enlightened. The will to live was not simply a prudent desire to survive; it was a will to power, constantly in conflict with other wills which in turn seek power. A living thing seeks above all else to discharge its strength, Nietzsche said; life itself is will to power; self preservation is simply one of the indirect and most frequent results.[1] Life could be best understood as a battlefield of wills, and will as an irrational force, inexorably egoistic and morally blind. From this basic force both good and evil arose. Its strength emerged as destructiveness as easily as creativeness; in fact, according to Nietzsche, the higher the type of energy a person possessed, the greater the improbability that it would turn out well. Artistic impulses, keen sensitivity, extended vision, religious temperament could not be seen as straightforward goods, for as manifestations of vitality they were tied not only in genesis but in character to madness, cruelty, criminality. A division between good and evil could not be drawn; the notion of a purely spiritual side of nature and mankind no longer had any application. Genius and creativeness, even in their brightest, most liberating forms, were not simple children of light, but were born of energies that are themselves amoral and which, in their unusually excessive strength, are akin to the dæmonic.

This is the basic world picture Mann inherited from Schopenhauer and Nietzsche, and his own moral development can be seen as a result of the tension between these philosophers' opposing recommendations of which value-systems should function within this world.

Mann's admiration for Nietzsche was boundless. He called him the greatest psychologist and moral critic of the age and noted the number of 'Freudian' perceptions scattered throughout his works. Nietzsche's psychology and moral criticism, however, did not provide Mann with what he sought, that is, a foundation and justification for an ethical culture based upon sympathy, reason and reverence for life. In fact, in the books Mann considered to be Nietzsche's best—*Beyond Good and Evil* and *Genealogy of Morals*—the philosopher's task was to argue against humanism and to expose the desire for such an ethical culture as cowardly and, according to his own value-system, immoral.

Nietzsche begins his criticism of conventional moral thought by saying he is not going to concern himself with truth, for he wishes to investigate the possibility that a higher and more fundamental value be ascribed to deception, selfishness and lust. The falsity of a moral judgement does not interest him; he cares only for what is life-enhancing, life-preserving, species-preserving, perhaps even species-creating. Initially this defiance of truth on behalf of life might appear as a humanist utilitarianism, but Nietzsche has nothing of the kind in mind. First, his arguments are not actually directed against true moral judgements but against the conventional moral axioms, taken as truths. The strength of a person, he suggests, should be measured according to how much truth he can endure; and in claiming to disregard truth himself, he underlines the way others disregard it, for Nietzsche is determined to pursue a line of moral argument even when it goes against ethical intuition. That a certain precept promotes happiness or what is ordinarily considered to be virtue is not, he points out, an argument for its truth. Truth might destroy; truth might favour conditions which promote pain; truth might be on the side of those who are, in conventional terms, considered evil. In short, he applies criteria which anyone would accept for the truth of empirical statements to common moral statements, and then asserts that the *possible* alternative—a true morality is in opposition to harmony and happiness—is fact. His presentation of this new morality, despite his logical sleight-of-hand, has an infectious energy, and is alarmingly intelligent.

Nietzsche's appreciation of life does not lead towards humanism because 'life-promoting' does not mean 'that which promotes humanity's well-being'. 'Life' is treated by Nietzsche as a value-laden word. It indicates a higher grade of vitality, and it is not humanism, not a morality which seeks to mitigate suffering or to defend the common person that will nourish this higher type of man, but a morality that will increase danger, privation and pain. Only as a result of suffering, Nietzsche claimed, has greatness been attained. To value human achievement is to value that which will promote it and therefore to value suffering and the assertion of strength. A morality based upon self-denial, humility and pity is a slave morality; it has utility only for the weak and the pathetic. Such a morality is developed and enforced by fear. Abject people advocate it because only in such weakness-breeding, comfort-seeking conditions can they survive. A morality in which the higher type of human could breed would attack the Christian specimen of 'the good man' because this 'good man' is a symptom of regression; his humility is a ploy to preserve the weak and destroy the strong. The current piety of self-abnegation and self-sacrifice is fear of truth, fear of the will to power—which is the essence of life—and therefore fear of life itself. Slave morality is the morality of the degraded masses who out of envy and terror try to deny the true excellence of that which would mock and destroy them. A higher morality, a master morality, does not concern itself with good as opposed to bad, but with noble as opposed to contemptible. Goodness, or nobility, in this morality denotes that which inspires and seeks to inspire fear and to destroy the weak. Master morality denies the Christian assumption that all souls are equal before God; it recognises ranks of souls, and the proud and self assertive men constitute the aristocracy. The aristocrat has duties of respect and tolerance only to his peers; towards others he can behave as he pleases. In fact, cruelty is a necessity, because there must be some outlet for the quarrelsome, exuberant spirits of these proud men—only when they are cruel to others will they be sufficiently healthy to be good friends to one another.

Nietzsche admits that glorification of vitality is dangerous, for exuberance is reckless and often barbaric; but, surely, he says, it is preferable to fear where one can admire than to be safe among pathetic slaves. After all, life itself is essentially appropriation, injury, destruction, suppression and exploitation of the alien and the weak.

These terms describe life; therefore they should not have derogatory connotations. His argument, ultimately, is psychological, rather than a Panglossian dictum: what is, should be. For he believed that not only is it evil, that is, opposed to life, to deny these impulses but also that such a denial would exacerbate the evil that is already in life. 'What ideas he has, what unnaturalness, what paroxysms of nonsense, what *bestiality of thought* erupts as soon as he is prevented just a little from being a *beast in deed* . . . Here is *sickness*, beyond any doubt, the most terrible sickness that has ever raged in man . . .'.[2] Cruelty is a necessary celebration of the spirit; only disease and regression can come of trust in man's weakest organ, his consciousness, and in persuading him to live in harmony with all men.

It is not surprising, then, that though Freud himself saw his own theories as incorporating a pessimistic assessment of mankind's rational adaptation to life, Mann found Freudian theory a refreshing contrast to Nietzsche and saw in it grounds for optimism.

Mann came to Freud late in his career. Some younger workers in the field of psychoanalysis were convinced, on the basis of the psychological interest he had revealed in *The Magic Mountain, Death in Venice*, and the Joseph novels, that he would be sympathetic to Freud's work. What struck him, naturally, was the emphasis on the unconscious as the largest part of the psyche and the description of the Id as the unorganised impulses and energies which provide the source of feeling and consciousness but which cannot be known directly and which can be understood only through the study of neurotic symptoms. None of this was unfamiliar to Mann. He had come across the idea in Schopenhauer, whose metaphysical system described the primacy of instinct over reason, with Will, or undirected and unspecified energy, as the core of life, and in Nietzsche, who exposed various examples of deception through repression and unconscious desire and who emphasised that health could be achieved through illness and that disease was an instrument of knowledge. Even Freud's insistence that the training of impulses is an exceedingly difficult task, that there can seldom be a proper balance between impulse and control, that the instincts are restrained either too much or too little, that civilisation only barely compensates for the pain caused by the repression it demands, that these unconscious human drives are the strongest human drives and that mankind is always threatened by his own bestiality, could not mitigate Mann's relief at finding a theory which both acknowledged the power of the unconscious and valued normality.

Mann said of Schopenhauer that his pessimism was derived from his vision of the intellect as a mere manifestation of the Will and its subservience to the amoral life-urge; but Freud claimed that these irrational impulses could be robbed of their energy by being made conscious through analytical procedure. This at least was Freud's hope; his studies were directed towards this end; and, therefore, psychoanalytic theory, while accomodating Nietzsche's picture of energy and restraint, was totally antipathetic to the glorification of the unconscious and to the worship of its life-promoting, death-wielding powers. Despite Freud's cynical prognosis of compromise between impulse and reason, Mann believed that psychoanalytic theory might form the cornerstone of a new humanism—a humanism which acknowledged without fear the power of those dark, unconscious forces and had with them a relation 'bolder, freer, blither, productive of a riper art than any possible in our neurotic, fear-ridden, hate-ridden world'.[3] Moreover, Freud's description of the domination of the unconscious could be taken as an argument against Nietzsche's belief that a master morality was necessary to preserve the strength of elemental impulses; for Freud's mental model showed that this mass of impulse did not need any protection, that it would survive and find expression no matter what. One can therefore wriggle out of Nietzsche's insistence that irrational energy should be celebrated and that suffering should be encouraged, by showing that attempts to tame and mitigate the effects of mankind's aggressive nature are bound to fail.

Psychoanalytic theory might be a forward-looking, healing, humanising science, but Mann nonetheless felt that it was not secure from the darker, backward tendencies within Romanticism. As a delver into the depths of mind, as a researcher in the psychology of instinct, Freud belonged to the nineteenth-century writers who were opposed to rationalism, intellectualism, classicism and who emphasised not consciousness but the irrational side of nature as the actual life-conditioning and life-giving element. Freud's attention is focused upon the dæmonic reality of the human psyche, on the primeval mass of unconscious excitations. Unlike a true Romantic, however, Freud does not despise consciousness because it is weak and shallow. His investigation of the deep and primitive aspect of mind is an attempt to protect intellect and its control. The voice of the intellect is low, Freud said, but it does not rest until it gets a hearing. Freud's science insists upon analysis of the unconscious as a means of amplifying the intellect's voice, and therefore it uses a Romantic, anti-rational view of humanity to serve enlightenment. Nonetheless, its model of the psyche, with the Id as the greater part, could be misused, and Mann therefore believed that while psychoanalysis might form the cornerstone of a new humanism, it must be enforced by a new morality, a morality that outlines a proper relationship with the total psyche. Often Mann leaves this notion of a new morality and a better world at the merest starting point; he speaks of a word of hope that cannot yet be uttered, that can only be stammered and barely understood, but which will lead to a glorious rebirth and transformation. His clearest definition of the desired ethical culture is offered in his 'Afterword' to Goethe's *Elective Affinities*; it is

> the deepest, most intuitively sympathetic relationship with nature, which is at the same time responsive to the higher command; with a moral conquest by which tragedy is resolved in love and issues in a transfiguration that instructs humanity to view as holy the unresolved tragedy of its own lot.[4]

In this definition Mann shows his affinity to Schopenhauer who, from his picture of a world forever battling against itself, derived sympathy as the main moral principle; for all wills are one Will, and the tragedy of all strife and suffering is one's own tragedy.

Mann discovered Schopenhauer in his early twenties, while he was writing *Buddenbrooks*. That novel too, as does every subsequent novel, bears the philosopher's stamp, though it is Schopenhauer as moralist and psychologist rather than as a dubious metaphysician who interested Mann. Like Nietzsche, who was at one time Schopenhauer's disciple, Schopenhauer saw all life as the will to assert itself and gain precedence or power. Through the illusion of the phenomenal world, the world as Idea, it appeared that numerous wills were in conflict, but reflection would discover that differentiation and individuality of this basic force were deceptions. The potential of all life, the force which emerges as life, both animate and inanimate, was a single, undifferentiated Will.

Since the world was Will, it was suffering; will indicates striving, and striving comes through defect, need, desire. Striving is the attempt to relieve suffering, but any relief gained is momentary; the will cannot achieve permanent satisfaction because striving is its essence. Usually even momentary satisfaction is difficult to achieve, but when objects of desire are easily gained, *ennui* results. This *ennui* is not to be taken lightly; Schopenhauer describes it as unspeakable despair. Thus life swings like a pendulum between pain and *ennui* until, inevitably, it reaches death; but even death does not provide release from the eternally striving Will. Individual life, individual will is deceptive appearance, and only individuality, the particular manifestation of the Will, is destroyed in death.

The highest good of the Will is a problematic notion, for the highest good would be complete and final satisfaction; yet, because the essence of the the Will is strife, satisfaction—the satisfaction of achieving the object of desire, so that desire is assuaged—is impossible. By default Schopenhauer then conceived the highest good as complete absence of willing. This absence can be attained by a contemplation of the world in which one's own will is disengaged from the eternal battle of wills. Momentarily, intellect, itself a manifestation of the Will, becomes master and indifferent to the world's toil. Schopenhauer defines this momentary disengagement as aesthetic contemplation, and as such it is episodic; it does not constitute a complete way of life or complete release from Will. With grace, however, a person can maintain total asceticism. Like the saint, he uses privation and suffering as a means of subduing desire. Over a period of time his will is truly calmed, and when he dies, his will has been so chastened that it remains calm even in death; but though death is desirable, there is no point in actively seeking it. The person who commits suicide asserts his will against the individual manifestation of life, not against the force which projects life; his will itself is unimpeded, and in such a case would continue to thrive after his phenomenal death. Only if a person achieves a total denial of his will, so that the world's battles do not interest him either for better or for worse, can he find the bliss of annihilation in death.

True reality is Will, the entire body of wills, an undifferentiated force; and from this theory Schopenhauer derives his notion of pity or sympathy as the basis of morality. A theory of morals without proof, Schopenhauer says, can effect nothing because it does not provide a motive; but a theory of morals which acts as a motive must do so by referring to self-love, and from self-love no action of moral worth can spring. Therefore no genuine virtue can be produced either by abstract knowledge or moral theory. In any case, he argues, the impulse to action, Will, is indifferent to the intellect and can be influenced only by emotion. One's emotions can be influenced by the perception of the world as one Will, for then one sees all suffering as one's own suffering, one sees the meaninglessness of strife and the foolishness of desire. Egoism is suppressed because the individual person, the individual manifestation of the Will, is seen to be illusory, and sympathy is aroused through the identification of all wills. As one views life as a whole, with all its cruel and purposeless striving, one is repelled, and this repulsion quiets one's will; it leads one away from the battle of life and makes it clear that our only hope lies in the annihilation of our will.

It is not surprising, in view of his notion of annihilation or will-lessness as the highest good, that Nietzsche turned away from his former mentor. Nietzsche hated nihilism, for it was a denial of the possible strength of man's spirit. He said that Schopenhauer's pessimism revealed a half-Christian, half-German narrowness and was under the spell of slave morality. A strong person would look upon the world's torments with courage rather than revulsion; in fact he would be delighted by the inexhaustible force of the Will and would want to celebrate its energy. Nietzsche's ideal man was one who would gladly relive the suffering of the world, and relive it again and again, for all eternity. The man with such courage would be the liberator, the Superman who triumphs over resignation. Delight in the cruelty of life takes one beyond Schopenhauer's nihilism; to celebrate horror is to embrace life.

Nietzsche despised Schopenhauer's assessment of pity as the basis of morality and as a possible anodyne to the Will. Such compassion was devoid of reverence and admiration for the force of life, and therefore was full of death. Nietzsche saw Schopenhauer's moral recommendation as the mark of a weak man who knew that he had to suffer and was afraid to suffer alone. He therefore generalised his condition and promulgated indiscriminate benevolence to improve his situation. Yet in a man devoted to a true morality, pity seems almost ridiculous, for the people who demanded pity were pathetic and unhappy; the man who truly pitied them would destroy them. To give them the kind of pity they requested, to help them survive, was dangerous, for such pity would naturally combine with nausea, as happened in Schopenhauer, and this combination of pity and nausea is nihilism. The strong could no longer maintain their pride and energy if they had to bow down to the weak. They would become ashamed of their special favour and they, too, would become men of misery and forced from their natural height by pity for the weak.[5]

Nietzsche's conception of the noble spirit was an aesthetic ideal, beyond good and evil, beyond what is ordinarily considered to be morality; and it was Nietzsche the aesthete who most frightened and enthralled Mann. Throughout the writer's life his attraction to Nietzsche was ambivalent, but his doubts reached a climax as he saw his favourite philosopher proclaimed a spokesman for National Socialism. Knowing how Nietzsche actually despised anti-Semitism and called it the most foul stupidity, Mann nonetheless saw how Nietzsche's thought was applicable to some of the tenets of Nazism. For in his vibrant, hypnotic style, with the quick, rich flow of his argument, Nietzsche had exposed the paleness of the safe and the tame and the mediocre as opposed to vigour and fearlessness. Mann saw that a master morality as outlined by Nietzsche would result if aesthetics was turned into a morality or into a political doctrine—if, that is, the aesthetic ideal was constituted by a Nietzschean definition of life and energy. To Mann, Schopenhauer's death-ridden atmosphere seemed healthier than Nietzsche's exuberant assertion of life. Schopenhauer's passivity and pessimism, though ostensibly against life, offered a far more acceptable way of life than one in which suffering was glorified.

Nevertheless, Mann could not turn his back on Nietzsche. He tried to defend him against the apparent implications of his own philosophy by insisting that Nietzsche should be viewed as an epilogue to the nineteenth century, as a critic of hypocritical propriety and complacent rationalism rather than as an advocate of the twentieth-century's barbarism. Mann would not see Nietzsche's praise of the ruthless and the assertive as a full-blooded moral error. Nietzsche had simply misjudged the strength of the human will; he had argued on its behalf because he feared that it might weaken under the influence of a shallow enlightenment; his mistake was to think there was any possibility that the will would become a lesser force than reason and caution. Mann did not deny the value and fascination of Nietzsche's concern with the dæmonic, but he denied that the dæmonic could ever be anything less than dangerous.

Mann's concern with impulses, their distortion and their menace, is allied to the tradition of Plato and Schopenhauer rather than to the traditional novel. He sometimes depicts characters of a type similar to Tolstoy's Karenin or Lawrence's Chatterley or Fontane's Baron Innstetten—characters whose impulses have been cheated by the way social pressures have worked upon them, so that they lose contact with their own emotions and therefore lack the capacity for expression and understanding. Helmut Institoris in *Doctor Faustus* comes closest to this type, but his main purpose is to serve as a parody, in his weakness, of aesthetic admiration of strength. The problem of emotional shallowness or frustration in an ordinary human setting has little claim upon Mann's attention. He is interested in the will, in that bed of impulses which, as Plato realised, is susceptible to aesthetic arousal; and it is in the artist that he centres his study of the will.

Throughout his life Mann was suspicious of the artist's function and intention. The artist's purpose should be to investigate moral and psychological truths, yet he dealt with illusion. The artist's glory was to create an appearance of reality, to make others believe in what they all knew to be imaginary. Mann wanted, in his fiction, to provide contemporary man with a contemporary ethical culture, but he was never certain about the wholesomeness of the imagination which conceived those would-be moral works. He saw an irony in presenting truths through elaborate illusion, and this irony often undercut the entire purpose. Moreover, the interest in illusion could easily overpower the moral interest, and Mann often presented the artist as a masquerader or a magician. Indeed, the work of the artist encourages an unfavourable balance, for his work involves sensitivity to beauty, and beauty, however spiritual in content or purpose, acts upon the senses in a way that tends to aggravate amoral impulses. The artist, the man detached from ordinary life, from the normal channels of emotion and personal connection that modify sensuality, is the man most susceptible to the destructive possibilities in beauty.

The artist's protean imagination and creativeness are at their best mixed goods. Mann's imagination thrived on their ambiguous value. He was suspect of anything that could fascinate, of anything that called forth an intense reaction; for in his Romantic aestheticism, fascination and intensity were the rudiments of artistic sensibility. His suspicion of impulse and sensuality is often indiscriminate. He revels in ambiguities, sometimes without giving sufficient content to the disturbing atmosphere. In spite of his admiration for Goethe and Tolstoy he could never adopt their supple measure of emotion and impulse; uncompromisingly he guarded against strong emotion because, as a disciple of Nietzsche and Schopenhauer, he saw emotion and sensuality as guides to the underworld of man's being. All vitality and enchantment, therefore, seemed to be on the side of the devil.

Throughout his novels and stories Mann struggled against the belief that the most interesting part of life was the dæmonic part, but the more he investigated the German Romantic tradition of death, soul-decay and grave-ridden ecstasy, the more he became entrenched in that tradition. His Romanticism sometimes appears in simple, child-like forms, such as delight in the narrow streets and towers of medieval German cities, in courtly lays of quests and tournaments, in tales of mediums and magicians; but these simple forms are only part of a sophisticated Romanticism that involves a fascination with disease and decay and a belief that forbidden investigations will reap precious knowledge. The Romantic imagination itself creates the peculiar, alluring darkness and proclaims it forbidden. The Romantic imagination craves spiritual visions, too, but it is satisfied only by a vision with enormous sensuous appeal, whose intensity makes ordinary life impossible. Mann knew that an acceptable morality could not be found amid these extremes, yet only these extremes seemed desirable.

For Mann the emotionality of Romanticism, and the only emotionality he knew, was nervous excitement and degeneration rather than personal liberation or deep-rooted connection. Rarely does he show any understanding of love as an emotion that can draw people together on terms of sympathy, care and tenderness. This limitation is clear from his earliest works. The characters in *Buddenbrooks* have no emotional history, just as Hans Castorp in *The Magic Mountain* and Aschenbach in *Death in Venice* have no emotional history, but only a single emotional episode which cannot be integrated into their lives. In this respect Mann, who both dreaded and longed for the mesmerisation of Wagner's music, is far more decadent than the composer; for though Wagner's emotionalism is often nervous, intense and sensuous, it is soul-rooted and capable of growth and fulfilment in a way that is foreign to Mann's images of passion. Mann's narrow vision artificially exacerbates the dangers of Romanticism, and makes passion seem a cold, deathly thing. He watches the course of passion with one eye, while the eye he lacks stares back at him with an opaque challenge.

If one is bounded by extreme Romanticism there is no way one can assert the value of humanism and life against the fascination of dissolution and death; for there is a melancholy masochism in Romantic suffering and longing which frustrates the will to life and happiness. Mann knew that the message of Wagner's *Tristan und Isolde* is not that love could be sublime were it not for the world. He knew that the opera's message could not be undercut by the prosaic denial that such a love in fact could maintain its fury and intensity if the world allowed it to have its way. He understood that the love in *Tristan* was a glorification of longing, and that this glorification was connected to a love of death, of a Schopenhauerian view of death as the realm of eternal, unbounded, ever-unsatiated longing. The masochism in Romanticism which frustrates the attainment of the posited object of desire is itself a powerfully seductive force; and though Mann tried, on behalf of life, to fight against it, he could never deny its magic.

Romanticism, as Mann saw and developed it, presented a further opposition to humanism. In its luxuriant torments erupt desires for only the ultimate in love and art and sensation. An acceptable morality, a morality based upon compassion and responsibility and justice, involves acceptance of a limiting reality. A humanist morality must engage in compromise because responsibility to other people involves relinquishment of other, more captivating possibilities; but the Romanticist will not sacrifice his aesthetic needs; instead, he will have death and grand gestures.

As Mann witnessed the decay of shallow bourgeois enlightenment and the rise of a barbaric morality which was to find its expression and confirmation in National Socialism, he tried to present the good and healthy possibilities of the German tradition from which this barbarism arose. In *Doctor Faustus* he brought together folk tales and a medieval atmosphere and a craving for forbidden knowledge and a nature governed by aesthetic principles alone; he hoped to bring Romanticism to its consummation and break through to a new, enlightened image. But his success was slim. The old Romantic images, the magnetism of death and disease and darkness, were too heavy for him; and, sinking downwards, he could only, like Wotan, proclaim that from the chaos a new, finer world based upon love and life, might someday emerge. He could not himself wear the Nibelung's ring of gigantic longing without being destroyed by its curse, but he hoped the impasse of his own fascination would eclipse the rich, vivid light in which he himself had portrayed Romanticism.

2 The Romantic Dilemma

The theme of the artist's alienation from life is a typically Romantic one. The artist is an outcast because his vision and sensibility are at odds with those of his society. In that respect alienation is thrust upon him; but he also cultivates and craves alienation, for the ordinary life of personal involvement and practical affairs is an enemy to his imagination; his vision is strengthened and vivified in solitude. At the same time, however, this alienation is painful; nor is it complete, and the tension between art and life is exacerbated by the demands made by reality and by the energy needed to get through the ordinary day.

The tension between art and life, though a familiar notion, does not have an obvious explanation. Art, after all, is an imaginative synthesis of life-possibilities; at its best it presents a significant and true picture of life. Indeed, the power and point of art is its investigation of the human world; and in Mann's case, even when he deals with the limited notion of art as beauty, and draws the opposition between art and life as the opposition between beautiful images on the one hand and drab reality on the other, his focus is upon human needs and human responses. The artist's imagination struggles with, not against life. His technical interests, which are interests in the means by which his vision can be expressed, are often solved by studying his subject matter—reality—more closely. It would seem, therefore, that the artist was more than usually committed to life, that his attachment to and participation in life would be enforced by his art.

There is, however, an important discrepancy between a commitment to the actual situations that ordinarily bind a person, the demands such a commitment makes upon his attention and his energy on the one hand, and the open-ended possibilities of life which the artist explores on the other. Exploration of these life-possibilities requires freedom from the facts which limit one's actual life; it requires the freedom to explore truths according to the impulses of one's imagination rather than according to the constraints of—often arbitrary—fact; it requires the freedom to attach one's imagination to one situation after another, as quickly and as completely as imagination can create them, and according to imagination's logic. The notion of a self that can exist without limitations becomes the notion of a self that is totally unbounded, undefined and, therefore, non-existent. Total possibility is annihilation, so that what seems to be reaching for everything is reaching towards nothingness. An enlightened mind would spot the deathliness and the absurdity in such a desire, but the art of the Romanticist presents the undeniable power of such yearning and expresses a death wish which is actually a wish for unlimited life. Furthermore, the energy demanded for the artist's imaginative synthesis seems to consume the energy that fuels personal affairs and practical actions. The opposition between the artist and life, therefore, is a matter of energy conservation.

Mann develops the theme of imagination's anatagonism to life with a Schopenhauerian model of the world and the various levels at which it is perceived, though it is the psychological aspect of Schopenhauer's philosophy, rather than the metaphysical world-picture that interested Mann. According to Schopenhauer only a narrow vision identifies the world of practical affairs and immediate aims with the real world. A more profound vision sees the phenomenal world merely as a manifestation of the Will, the single gigantic force, the fundamental reality. To contemplate the world aesthetically, to disengage oneself from immediate desire and immediate action, is to reflect upon the true nature of the world. It is the man of action, the man of practical affairs and of emotions, the man bound to 'normal' life, whose vision is unreal.

Schopenhauer saw music as the most direct expression of the Will within the phenomenal world, for music expresses energy, movement and feeling without reference to specific subjects and objects. Mann shared this sense of music's special power and its special relation with the non-conceptual, animating core of life, but he saw all imagination, too, as allied to this force. And since it is the force which denies the reality of immediate and individual life, it is also the force of death. The artist's penchant for death stems not only from his desire to escape the solitude and alienation which his work both thrusts upon him and demands; death, according to Mann's Romantic conception, is the substance of his imagination and, as he sees it, the substance of life. Schopenhauer's metaphysical view of death as Will released from its limiting, phenomenal manifestations became for Mann an image of imagination's psychology. The more one is in sympathy with this vital but individually destructive force, the more pronounced are one's aesthetic sensibilities, the less concern one has for the 'real world'

of personal and practical involvement. The profundity of imagination makes it impossible to believe in the petty meaning life has to
offer. Mann's first full-length novel, *Buddenbrooks*, published in 1901
when he was twenty-six years old, is subtitled 'The Decline of a
Family'; and the mercantile family's decline is the development of its
artistic sensibility.

Security and complacency dominate the opening scene of the book
as Johann Buddenbrook, the founder of the family's grain firm,
smugly and ironically enjoys his granddaughter Tony's recitation of
her catechism. God has created the child and all other living creatures;
this divinely formed world is a safe and simple place which rewards
the burghers for their hard work and which the burghers can control
quite satisfactorily if they are sensible businessmen. Heavy pastries,
heavy gold dishes, good heavy food, rich silver plate, thick draperies,
secure business reputations and family traditions define their world of
health and contentment. Consul Johann's strong hold upon life is
emphasised when, for one moment, he is distracted by sounds of a
flute and harmonium, but then shakes off the enchantment to return
to his duties as host of the housewarming. When the third generation
Buddenbrook, Tom, marries a violinist, the practical strain in the
family comes to an end.

The dramatic structure of the novel is based upon the tension
between artistic sensibility and life-orientation, but the 'life' which
Mann posits in opposition to imagination is comically depleted life.
Life is the collection of physical objects as symbols of wealth and
business success. It is social position and family tradition—tradition as
public display. The comedy of manners is a tremendous success, and
in itself places the novel among Mann's best. Indeed, the characters
have a vividness which is uncommon in his later works, and this
vividness redeems them as characters, despite their empty lives and
ambitions. The scene in which Tony's parents try to persuade her to
marry Grünlich because they believe, very mistakenly, he will be an
asset to the family and to the firm, is one among many examples of the
characters' shallowness, selfishness and confusion drawn lightly and
pointedly, with their complacency balanced by the ruthless social
forces that are outstripping their simple burgher mentality:

'How nice to find you still here, for once, Papa,' [Tony] said as
she held her egg in her napkin and opened it with her spoon.

'But today I was waiting for our slug-a-bed,' said the Consul. He
was smoking a cigar and tapping on the table with his folded

newspaper. His wife finished her breakfast with her slow, graceful motions, and leaned back in the sofa.

'Tilda is already busy in the kitchen,' continued the Consul, 'and I should have been long since at work myself, if your mother and I had not been discussing a serious matter that concerns our little daughter.'

Tony, her mouth full of bread and butter, looked first at her father and then at her mother, with a mixture of fear and curiosity.

'Eat your breakfast, my child,' said the Frau Consul. But Tony laid down her knife and cried, 'Out with it quickly, Papa—please.' Her father only answered, without for one moment ceasing to play with his newspaper, 'Eat your breakfast first.'

So Tony drank her coffee and ate her egg and bread and green cheese silently, her appetite quite gone. She began to guess. The fresh morning bloom disappeared from her cheek, and she even grew a little pale. She said 'Thank you' for the honey, and soon after announced in a subdued voice that she had finished.

'My dear child,' said the Consul, after a further moment's silence, 'the matter we desire to talk over with you is contained in this letter. He was now tapping the table with a big blue envelope instead of the newspaper. 'To be brief: Bendix Grünlich, whom we have learned to regard as a good and charming man, writes to me that during his stay here he has conceived a strong inclination for our daughter and he here makes a formal request for her hand. What does my child say?'

[. . .] 'I don't know him the least little bit,' Tony said in a dejected tone, wiping her eyes on the little white batiste serviette, stained with egg. 'All I know is, he has golden-yellow side whiskers, and a flourishing business . . . .' Her upper lip, trembling as she wept, had an expression indescribably touching.

With a movement of sudden tenderness the Consul jerked his chair nearer hers and stroked her hair, smiling.

'My little Tony, what could you possibly know about him? [. . .] You are a child, with no eyes yet for the world, and you must trust other people who mean well by you [. . .] Meanwhile I shall write an answer to Herr Grünlich's letter, without either consenting or refusing. There is much to be considered.—Well, is that agreed? What do you say?—And now Papa can go back to his work. Adieu, Betsy.'

'Auf Wiederschen, my dear Jean.'

'Do take more honey, Tony,' said the Frau Consul, who sat in

her place motionless, with her head bent. 'One must eat enough.'
                    Part 3, chapter 2, pp. 82–4[1]

The scope of the Buddenbrooks' emotional life is fully covered by
Tony's slight bout of paleness, by the indescribably touching
trembling of her upper lip, by her father's sudden tenderness that
contains no understanding, and by the mother's belief that more
honey will compensate Tony for her unappealing husband. The
parents' knowledge of Grünlich as a good and charming man is based
upon forged business records and references granted by creditors who
have been promised payment upon receipt of the Buddenbrook
dowry. The Buddenbrooks' assessment of the world as a straightforward place which can be governed by hard work and good sense is
overtaken by Grünlich's schemes.

All the old burgher families of the Buddenbrook type decline
while the new, unscrupulous merchants thrive. The latter are
untroubled by sentiment and aesthetic sensibility. Their children,
Hanno Buddenbrook's schoolmates, are interested only in physical
bravado, crude jokes and the glory of the fatherland. These boys,
with their arrogance and conceit, clearly belong to the generation
that will encourage Nazism. These boys despise the arts, and Mann
has not, at this point, drawn any connection between aesthetic and
political interests. The artistocratic class, which declined while the
burgher class was still strong and which has now accepted its failure in
the practical world, has emerged as a new type, as the artistic class,
while the burghers flounder amid the mingling of their practical
ambitions and their aesthetic natures.

Like Nietzshe, Mann did not believe that the surviving specimen
was the best possible specimen of man. A practical, shallow
consciousness had the strength of the herd behind it and could
therefore defeat the fragile but more valuable imagination; but unlike
Nietzsche—and this is characteristic of Mann's portrayal of the
artist—he did not see the man who undermined the values of the herd
as a strong man. Nietzsche believed that eventually the higher man's
resentment at the denial of his imagination would prove creative; in
the decay of the old order, the higher man would create new values
with his abundance of life and strength. For Nietzsche life and
strength were allied to creativeness. Mann, however, lacked a
thoroughly positive evaluation either of life or creativeness. His
comedy of manners does not simply register the stupidities and
confusions of the patrician class; it provides a definition of life which

offers a poor alternative to imagination.

Nonetheless, in the first seven parts of the novel, artistic sensitivity is no more robust or valuable than the burghers' impoverished 'life'. The first deviant from a purely practical way of life is Gotthold Buddenbrook, Johann Senior's child by his first wife, whom he married out of love rather than prudence. Gotthold, is in turn, married for love and disgraced the family by his marriage, and his half-brother Johann Junior, reveals an imaginative strain in his sentimental love for the family record book and his pietism. Christian Buddenbrook's imagination, the most pronounced of his generation, is totally morbid, debilitating, melancholic. It is not until Hanno, the last male Buddenbrook, that, vaguely, the imagination reaches towards something of real value.

The tension between art and life, then, is presented primarily as that between the bland, dull-witted and insensitive on the one hand, and the morbid, nervous and idle on the other. The problem is presented as an emotional battle, a battle between conflicting impulses, rather than a Nietzschean battle of values. The poverty of the alternatives, therefore, is less important in this novel than the struggle itself.

Tom Buddenbrook is the focus for the destructive work of the imagination upon ordinary, healthy life. He believes he can use his imagination to serve the family's reputation, but his admiration of elegance is at odds with the solid, substantial, tasteless regard for wealth that had served the previous generation so well. The new light and airy house he builds in Fischer Lane wastes the family's capital on mere appearance. He designs it according to aesthetic principles and thus it lacks the spirit upon which the family's survival depends. He is unable to keep pace with current business methods because he seeks inspiration from some ideal, rather than from reality. He is indecisive and bewildered when faced with the need to make practical decisions, for there is no meeting point between his imagination and the world.

Soon after the death of Consul Johann, Tom's father, Mann mentions that Tom's hands are different from the typically broad Buddenbrook hand, that they have well-groomed, oval fingernails and make little gestures of shrinking sensitivity and painful reserve. His physical constitution, too, is weak; the blue veins show clearly at his narrow temples, and he has a tendency to chills. At forty-eight he looks and feels like an old man; yet, like an artist, he believes in the power of appearance, and hopes to restore his energy by preserving an immaculate exterior. Aware of his inward dissolution, his life becomes that of an actor. Every hour he has to withdraw to groom himself again; and, since his essence has become his appearance, he must always have the spotlight upon himself; to have his appearance ignored is, for the actor, annihilation.

Imagination wills the destruction of practical life, and Tom is helpless in face of this will. He believes that sense and sensibility can be combined, but, in Mann's view, imagination will not rest until it is supreme. Only when imagination is self-sufficient, only when the significance of reality—other than as fodder to the imagination—is denied, can the imaginative person thrive, as Felix Krull thrives. In the case of an imaginative person who values a practical life, the conflict results in inward dissolution; there is a total split between what he finds attractive and what he values. This impasse creates a sympathy with death; for in death the conflict is resolved; in death one is freed from practical striving and one merges with the eternal force, the eternal longing which in all Mann's works is allied to the imagination.

When Tom sees his traditional values—the continuation of the family line and the progress of the business—as a dead end, when his only son proves to be totally unsuited to business affairs, when even his wife deserts him for music, he finds a volume of metaphysical philosophy inside a drawer of a garden table. For the most part, this volume reads like the third book of Schopenhauer's *The World as Will and Idea*, in which the reality of death is denied. In Schopenhauer's view, generation and death are equal manifestations of the Will; and wherever Will exists, life exists, for the Will is life. When the individual dies, the Will is freed from the deception and limitation of individuality; it wakes again in its eternal, primal aspect.

Tom Buddenbrook feels a tremendous release as he confronts this metaphysical view. For a few hours he is able to see the unreality of the merchants' ambitions and the pettiness of his failures. Since his release is the same sort of negation of 'life' that music, as the strongest representative of the imagination, provides, it is not surprising that the language in which Tom's metaphysical ecstasy is described, is similar to the language Mann uses to describe other musical experiences. Tom feels a strange, pressing but sweet intoxication that renders him incapable of consecutive thought, yet which seems to flood his mind with light. He is welcoming the power of the imagination, which destroys him, as it will destroy Hanno and Aschenbach and Mario.

The joyful expansion, the life-assertion Tom sees in his volume of metaphysics, is not actually found in Schopenhauer. Indeed, the philosopher lamented the fact that individual death was not actual death. He recommended complete suppression of one's will, so that one's individual death might more plausibly be an end to that carefully starved will. For only in annihilation of one's will is there rest from pain, deprivation, yearning on the one hand, and ennui and despair on the other. In the volume Tom Buddenbrook finds, however, the Will's passion and indestructibility are embraced with Nietzschean energy. He reflects that he has been mistaken in worrying about the survival of the family name and of the family firm. He had been accustomed to supposing that only the survival of these would ensure his own immortality, but this metaphysical argument convinces him that he will live on in all those who discover the elemental, eternal Will in their own selves; he will live on in all those who say 'I'—especially in those who say 'I' potently, fully, gladly. In death, as he merges with the Will, he will realise the fundamental and valuable part of his self. It is a vision based not as much upon a metaphysical supposition of the world's constitution, as upon a way of life. Tom sees his capacity for vitality and life-confidence as the measure of his true worth. He sees the possibility of kinship with other people who share this power and conviction. He does not discover a new metaphysics as much as a new morality—a morality in light of which his commercial ambitions seem unreal, unreal in the sense of being shallow and unimportant. He discovers his share in a humanity and joy that will never be destroyed as long as any life remains, and this participation satisfies him as an image of his own immortality.

Tom, however, cannot sustain this vision. In the morning he feels ashamed of the previous night's extravagance, and he never returns to the volume. The cruel failure of his hold upon this positive image of death can be seen in Tom's actual death. Mann shows the seedy-looking Senator leaving the assembly early, continually flexing his mouth as though to swallow an unpleasant liquid. In a grotesquely comic scene the dentist tries to extract the tooth that has been bothering Tom, but the crown of the tooth breaks, which means that the four roots will have to be extracted separately. On his way home, Tom collapses in the street. Mann's emphasis on the ugliness of his death—his mud-spattered clothes, the pool of blood lying beside his mouth, the abrasions on his face—confines it to the petty world of respectable appearances and business dealings in which Tom has failed. Nor is there any personal connection that might redeem this sordid picture. His wife Gerda turns her face away in disgust as he is carried upstairs. His sister Tony tries to uplift the wake with a hymn, but in mid-phrase she forgets the words, and the sentimental effect becomes an excruciating embarrassment.

In *Buddenbrooks* life is defined as business and social concerns. Tom's single redemption was a denial of the importance of life, and though this denial carried an atmosphere of vitality, it was allied to death. In Schopenhauer's metaphysics, the vision of the personal will as a part of one Will, the vision which for a few hours entranced Tom, is a starting point of morality; for in acknowledging the ultimate reality as a single Will, the conflict of desires is seen to be absurd and one sees oneself as the subject of all suffering—therefore one seeks to mitigate suffering. For Tom, however, the sympathy is more selective; he identifies only with those who say 'I' potently and gladly. More importantly, the sympathy he discovers through this identification has no relevance to his attitude towards the people around him. The metaphysics offers a release from concern for those people rather than a deepening of his sympathy with them. Any happiness of a value greater than complacency, it seems, can only be found apart from immediate life. There can be no resolution between practical, active life and reflection or imagination because the practical and immediate world is shallow, whereas imagination seeks vision and meaning. Mann presents the two in utter opposition, one destructive of the other.

Human emotion and the need for human connection might provide an area of possible resolution between the appeal of the imagination and the limiting bonds of life. If one made the highly plausible assumption that people have certain emotional needs, that at least part of human meaning is realised in close personal relations, and that emotions are in some way tied to the imagination, that the kind of stimulus either passion or family affection provides is akin to the expansion and intensity promised by the imagination, then we have a starting point for resolution. The imagination is a vagrant; it cares nothing for actual commitment but only for that which will present the most satisfying image. Personal ties demand responsibility and commitment; people, generally, want to be connected to others, and this connection limits other possibilities and gives the actual emotional situation a meaning which compensates for the loss of freedom. If emotion is understood to be real and valuable, then imagination's need for meaning, intensity and communion would have some fulfilment in life. Imagination's values would have some possible realisation in the actual, immediate world, though to achieve this realisation imagination's vagrancy would have to be controlled by a limiting reality.

In most of Mann's writing, however, the need for human connection is ignored and the value of emotion is denied. The bridging of the gap between life and imagination is not seen as something which our own emotional needs render necessary but rather as something which is prudent for social survival. The gap is so great, in short, because there is no convincing reason to bridge the gap, so long as one prefers the profundity of image as opposed to the shallowness of life. Love is, *prima facie*, on the side of imagination; it is not an emotion which the sturdy strain of Buddenbrook values, and the first sign of 'bad blood' in the family—of character, that is, not totally committed to practical issues—is Gotthold, who is the product of a love match (Johann Senior was married to Gotthold's charming mother for one year, but in Mann, love and health do not go together, and she died in giving birth) and who, in turn, disgraces the family in his choice of a love-mate. In subsequent works Mann presents passion as a feverish aggravation of the imagination, as an emotion which isolates one from the world rather than as one which binds one to it; his notion of passion is not desire for contact or connection with another person but rather a longing to be steeped in one's own longing and to be destroyed by it. In *Buddenbrooks* love works against practical success, but it is too weak to be anything more than a nuisance. Emotional compulsion in the family line is incipient and frail; it emerges as little more than stupidity. Gotthold's clandestine love-marriage is never presented directly, but the grotesque offspring indicate that the marriage does not provide fulfilment. When Christian is finally able, after the deaths of his mother and brother, to marry the woman he loves, the woman who, he believes, will give him the affection and respect his family deny him, she commits him to an institution and appropriates all his money. Even young Tony, who is so thoroughly committed to being a Buddenbrook that she fails miserably whenever she tries to join another family, is tempted by love to deviate from purely practical considerations; and in this case, too, love turns out to be pathetic and illusory. Morten blurts out his request that Tony wait for him until he takes his medical degree; she gives her promise and they seal the agreement with a kiss: 'Then they stared in different directions into the sand, and both felt the utmost shame'.[2]

It is plausible that in this situation the initial spark of love did die and leave nothing but shame. However, Mann is seldom able to present a more robust view of love. (Even Aschenbach, despite the fervour of his feelings, is afraid to speak to Tadzio lest he be disillusioned.) When Pierre proposes to Hélène in *War and Peace*, Pierre's shame indicates the emotional hollowness of this particular situation; but Mann's portrayal of the nervousness and distaste in emotional expression is a comment not on one particular situation, but on emotion itself. The obvious irony of these love situations (for Morten becomes a successful doctor and therefore would have been, both in social and financial terms, a better match for Tony and the Buddenbrook family than was Grünlich, for whom she forsakes Morten; and Christian's love-marriage, which he believes will shield him from the loneliness he suffers within his own family, results in total isolation) is not an example of Mann's notorious irony of ambiguity. He does not, in *Buddenbrooks*, present love as an emotion which appears to be utterly satisfying but which actually is destructive, or which destroys even as it satisfies; he simply shows love to be shallow. Imagination, even as it undermines practical life, seems to realise some human need; but in this novel love is a mere mistake. The irony in these love situations does not emerge from a balance of good and evil or from a sense of good within evil; it is the comic irony which emerges as the characters move towards their own downfall while they see themselves as cleverly avoiding it.

This reductive portrayal of love is one aspect of Mann's slender understanding of any interpersonal emotion. When a marriage is successful as a financial and social arrangement, Mann seems to believe that only social and financial issues are relevant to a description of the marriage. Johann Junior married Elizabeth Kröger when his father tapped him on the shoulder and pointed to the daughter of the wealthy aristocrat. From that moment, Mann says, Johann Junior honoured his wife as the mate entrusted him by God. These remarks constitute the total emotional story. And when Johann Senior's wife dies, Mann says, 'She had never given him either a great joy or a great sorrow; but she had with good breeding played her part beside him for many long years—and now, likewise, her life was ebbing away'.[3]

It is not the lack of love between married people that is implausible but the lack of any feeling whatsoever. It is difficult to believe that Tony does not even hate Grünlich after living with him and bearing his child and being cheated and ignored by him. Her revulsion is not developed beyond the initial distaste; it is simply part of the comedy. Consistently Mann refuses to give his characters an emotional dimension.

Sometimes Mann's failure to focus personal relationships results not only in an incomplete presentation of character but also in an inconsistent one. Mann says of Tom and his wife Gerda that there was not much love in their feelings for one another, though there was a correct, respectful politeness due not to estrangement but to a peculiar, silent, profound mutual knowledge. This assertion, however, cannot be accepted in light of his other descriptions of the couple. It is possible that Gerda, with her cool, reserved sensibility has some deep, silent knowledge of Tom, though there is no indication that she has any respect for his business concerns nor that she has any understanding of his confused battle with imagination. It is inconceivable, however, that Tom has a deep knowledge of her. Mann, in fact, emphasises Tom's bewilderment in face of his wife's absorption in music. He feels threatened and utterly at a loss when she shares that interest with another man because he knows he cannot understand her. The couple exhibit a marked lack of mutual respect in their conflicting attitudes towards their son's musical inclinations and lack of business acumen; and there is no sign of regard for her husband in the way Gerda turns her face away in disgust as Tom's body is carried into the house.

Nonetheless, it would be misleading to call Mann an insensitive writer. His awareness of feeling comes alive in the tension his characters suffer between life and imagination. His portrayals of isolation, despair, ecstasy, alienation and fear of death, are unrivalled. In such cases the characters are not reduced to social and financial considerations. Their physical defects become unimportant, and however ironic the situation, sympathy is not undermined—as it is in his love situations—by the sense that their emotions are ridiculous. Frau Consul Buddenbrook, Tom's mother, has been presented as her husband's proper but insignificant partner, as a well-meaning but ineffective mother—in short, she is nothing more, emotionally speaking, than a moderately competent Buddenbrook, until she becomes ill; and alone, outside the family structure, she struggles with death. Then, brilliantly, her personality is given a new dimension. She is no longer the character in the comedy of manners, defined by the solid expensive objects in her house, she is a force battling bravely against terror and decay. This new dimension is not inconsistent with Mann's earlier presentation of her character, but brings out the value in what had previously seemed mere shallowness. The Frau Consul's fight against death is one aspect of her commonplace healthiness. Her consciousness had once been bound by practical interests (with the exception of an excessively religious sentimentality which was probably responsible for the unhealthy, imaginative traits in her children) but now the respect for survival emerges as a positive force. She has a naïve, robust hatred of illness, and therefore her soul will not give in to disease. The disease, therefore, has to break her down both physically and spiritually. Her symptoms are described in cold, ugly detail; but the blood-impregnated mucus she brings up with her cough, the failing digestion, the bed sores that grow worse and will not heal, her sunken, roving eyes, her delirium, are not here—as are similar symptoms in *The Magic Mountain*—subjects of fascination. Rather, they show the battle between life and death, a battle whose cruelty is far more vivid than in the Berghof Sanatorium, where dissolution is always welcome. When Frau Consul's healthy spirit is destroyed she struggles towards death, but not because she has become corrupt in the way Hans Castorp or Aschenbach are corrupt. Her desire for death is not a Romantic yearning but a desire to escape useless pain.

Certainly this breakdown of the healthy spirit into a craving for death is a model of the Buddenbrook family itself, with the once healthy, naïve practical consciousness passing through a variety of painful spiritual diseases until, in Hanno, death is the only possible resolution; but Frau Consul's death gives some dignity and significance to the will to survive which so often in the novel is presented as petty and shallow. Frau Consul faces death and fights it, whereas imagination faces it and is hypnotised by it.

Mann is similarly sensitive to the sufferings of Tom and Hanno, but always the emotions he sympathetically explores are those which define a character's isolation and his rejection of the ordinary world. In subsequent works Mann treats the longing to escape with careful irony. The sweetness of release is set against the necessity of self-control and commonplace existence, but in *Buddenbrooks*, escape from the merchants' practical life—though the only escape is death—is welcomed with only very slender modification. Tom's metaphysical ecstasy which denies the reality of his business worries and which puts him in contact with all those who say 'I' potently and gladly, is based upon a vision of death, and his joyful sense of release from boundaries and barriers is the sense that is he approaching death. Music, too, the vehicle of his son Hanno's release, is a path to death.

Schopenhauer believed that music was the highest art form because it was the most direct expression of the Will that could appear in the phenomenal world. Music itself, as sound, is of course pheno-menal, but it does not depend upon concepts as do other art forms. Music is a first-hand representation of the Will, for it expresses longing, strife, desire, and despair without reference to particular manifestations of these emotions. Other art forms generally refer to the world in its phenomenal aspect; for the painter, sculptor and poet, the world he represents is the phenomenal world, the world of individual things—trees, bodies, people, subjects and objects of desire and need. Therefore, art forms other than music are representations of representations of the Will, and are therefore less immediate and powerful than music.

Though Mann shares Schopenhauer's assessment of music's power and believes that the power depends upon its special access to the deepest energies of the psyche, he does not use Schopenhauer's metaphysical argument. After all, Schopenhauer concludes from the argument with which he supports music's claim to superiority, that opera, in which individual people and situations are represented, is the lowest form of music. For Mann, however, this musical form was particularly compelling; it is the meeting-place of the Will's prime representative and the actor, the man who values illusion more than reality.

The imaginative strain in the Buddenbrook line—which appears in Consul Johann Junior's love for the family record book, Tom's admirations for elegance and his compulsion to keep up his appearance as a successful merchant, Christian's hypochondria and passion for the theatre—has its final development in Hanno's love for music, especially for Wagner. The doors to life are now closed tightly, and imagination finds so perfect a satisfaction that it can never again turn to practical existence.

Mann's attitude towards music is inextricably connected to his attitude towards Wagner. It is through the arguments between his mother and the Church organist Edmund Pfühl about the value of Wagner's music that Hanno begins his musical education. The organist holds the fond and foolish belief that music is an extremely intellectual art. As he plays works which uphold this belief his face reveals

foolish tenderness, rapture and revelry, and his gaze would rest upon the sanctified distance, as though he saw there the ultimate logicality of all events, issuing in reality. This was the musician's look; vague and vacant precisely because it resides in the kingdom

of a purer, profounder, more absolute logic than that which shapes
our verbal conceptions and thoughts.

Part 8, chapter 6, p. 389

The notion that the more profound and absolute logic of music is an
intellectual and holy logic is denied throughout Mann's works. In
The Magic Mountain the humanist Settembrini warns against music's
power and suggests that music always be tempered by the rationality
and morality of literature; in *Doctor Faustus* the intellectual rigour of
music is used to express the irrational and the barbaric; and in the
novella *Tristan* Mann presents the absurd yet magical power of
Wagner's great romantic opera and shows that power to be a death-
influence—for to look upon the deepest and most recalcitrant
yearnings of the psyche is to long to give way to them, and this
submission to the inner darkness is death.

Edmund Pfühl, however, claims that Wagner's compositions are
not music. After playing twenty-five bars of a piano arrangement of
Tristan und Isolde he proclaims the work to be chaos, demagogy,
blasphemy, madness, a perfumed fog shot through with lightning.
His account of the composition is correct; his mistake is to say that it is
not music; for blasphemy, madness and demagogy are precisely what
Mann takes music to be. The sheer strength of its effect makes it
unanswerable to reason; it frees one from the constraints of life but
dominates with its own power. Music is allied to the deepest longings,
the continuous longings of the psyche which, when active, become
aggressive and cruel, and, when passive, become a longing for
nothingness, a longing for death. In *Buddenbrooks* the longings are
passive, and the effect of Wagner's music becomes both an intolerable
burden and a most profound satisfaction. Hanno's love for the music
saps his energy and his concentration. He is incapable of doing his
school work—he has no belief in the reality of his school work—in
face of the prospect of a performance of *Lohengrin*. Throughout the
week Hanno looks forward to it,

And then the bliss became reality. It came over him with all
the enchantment and consecration, all its secret revelations and
tremors, its sudden inner emotion, its extravagant, unquenchable
intoxication [. . .] Again he learned that beauty can pierce one
like a pain, and that it can sink profoundly into shame and a
longing despair that utterly consumes the courage and energy
necessary to the life of the everyday. His despondency weighed

him down like mountains, and once more he told himself, as he had
done before, that this was more than his own individual burden of
weakness that rested upon him: that this burden was one which he
had borne upon his soul from the beginning of time, and must one
day stifle it.

Part 11, chapter 2, pp. 546–7

This description of Hanno's response is based upon a Schopenhauerian model of individual suffering as a fraction of the universal
suffering Will—an eternal force from which has emerged, for a
limited period, the manifestation one normally identifies as one's self.
This model is superimposed upon Mann's own highly problematic
response to Wagner, which registers a problem of the imagination in
general. According to Schopenhauer, aesthetic contemplation lifts
one momentarily above the toil of the Will; for Schopenhauer,
aesthetic contemplation was a momentary release from longing,
desire and deprivation. For Mann, however, though aesthetic
contemplation releases one from the commonplace conflict and
assertion of wills, it subjects one more nakedly and more profoundly
to the dark and eternal forces. The asceticism which Schopenhauer
advocated as the only way to resolve the pain of willing is stood on its
head; for in Mann aesthetic response leads to a love of longing and
pain, a hunger for longing itself, a desire to have the boundaries of
individual life dissolved so that one is free to merge with ultimate and
eternal yearning and suffering. The logical difficulties in this notion
do not diminish the fascination and the desire for release and mystical
consummation. A self dissolved of all boundaries and individuality
cannot find satisfaction because it cannot exist; yet extreme emotions
and extreme longings have an impetus which explains this death
wish. Such a wish is not dependent upon a metaphysical view of
individual dissolution and transformation after death; rather, the
metaphysical view is interesting as an expression of a psychological
craving—a craving for an ultimate and extreme perfection of
emotion and longing, a craving for a Romantically conceived
perfection of desire and impulse. This the daylight world will not
allow, and the dissatisfaction with the daylight world becomes a
confused, compelling desire for death, where death is seen as
providing the perfection life denies.

The Romantic imagination will not compromise. Its greatest
goods are intensity and beauty and longing to merge with the object
of desire. These goods thrive upon desire; the Romanticist sees in

longing the best intensifier of beauty and emotion; therefore the Romanticist yearns for longing. Ordinary life must be rejected because commonplace distractions and ebbings of mood disperse intensity and offer compensatory satisfactions. The Romanticist values eternal longing, and longing can be eternally sustained only when emotion and concentration are held in suspension. This desire for suspension and the hope of eternal intensity becomes a heavenly, and therefore a deathly, vision. Wagner's *Tristan und Isolde*, with its conception of death as the only power great enough to contain a love consisting of supreme longing, is perhaps the boldest Romantic assertion of death as fulfilment, but in Wagner's other operas, too, with the exception of *Die Meistersinger*, longing and stasis are peculiarly and compellingly combined. Furthermore, his works both express profound, prerational impulses and have an elemental energy—feelings and energies which are, in normal, social life, modified or suppressed. The music's appeal to these (usually) suppressed impulses can appear as a disturbing attack upon the socialised consciousness.

These strangely juxtaposed effects of Wagner's music are apparent in the history of Nietzsche's attitudes towards the composer. In his early essay, *The Birth of Tragedy from the Spirit of Music* he saw *Tristan und Isolde* as an expression of the world's deepest impulses and the most elemental forces of life, as an expression of love and pain and sorrow almost too great for the individual soul to bear. He saw the opera as a renewal of the tragic vision, for it had the strength and courage and elemental passion and inexorable view of suffering necessary to such a vision. Later Nietzsche saw Wagner's music as a gigantic form of weakness, as the epitome of fear of life and rejection of true, passionate suffering. In his tirade against the composer, Nietzsche said that he wanted music that would quicken his flow of blood, that would make him exuberant and would lead to dancing. Nietzsche wanted music that was an overflow of the life-spirit, whereas the pronounced and anguished longing heard in Wagner's music showed absence of life and love of death. It made him feel sluggish and depressed. He continued to acknowledge the music's hypnotic power, but said that those in favour of life and active energy must turn away from it.

Though Mann understood and even admired Nietzsche's hatred of the composer, he saw this rejection as a side-stepping of the problem. He agreed that a firm moral line, on behalf of life, would condemn this music that so diminished life-energy with its gigantic longings and sensual fascination, but such a moral position would enforce an asceticism intolerable to the Romanticist. It was in imagination, in aesthetic creation and aesthetic response, that Mann found the greatest satisfaction and the greatest meaning. If imagination was so profoundly moved by the notions of death and longing, then this response indicated some human need which should be resolved rather than ignored. If one treated Wagnerian enchantment simply as a drug-effect which one should avoid to stay healthy, then one suppressed the fact of imagination's power. The obviously mixed good of this power was problematic, but it could not, on that ground, be dismissed.

In *Buddenbrooks* Mann did not offer any resolution to the opposition between imagination and life. He merely stated the opposition and left it at an impasse. The only fulfilment imagination could have was in death. The chapter that follows the detailed account of Hanno's love for Wagner constitutes nothing more than a description of the course of typhoid fever. The despondency, lethargy and delirium which characterise the disease are a counterpart of his response to music. The longing Hanno hears in Wagner's *Lohengrin* and which he suffers as his own, stifles him; but the life alternatives presented in this novel are so impoverished that this passive acceptance of death commands not only sympathy but also approval. It is against this obviously limited vision which Mann's humanistic principles subsequently struggle.

In *Buddenbrooks* the imagination which opposes life is passive; it is overwhelmed by music or beauty or the theatre, and can find no expression for its sensibility. Furthermore, all the Buddenbrooks are passive as imagination destroys them, and Hanno, whose sensibilities are the most pronounced, is bewildered by his alienation. He has a school friend, however, Kai, Count Mölln, who has reached a stage in aesthetic sensibility beyond the Buddenbrooks' life-negating impasse. Kai's aristocratic family has accepted its economic decline, and with the strength of aristocratic assurance, Kai is indifferent to the ordinary world's rejection. Kai knows he will be a writer, and the ability to make use of his imagination and to understand his alienating position, makes it possible for him to survive.

Tom Buddenbrook realises that imagination which has no creative outlet will become trivial and morbid. He says of his brother Christian:

Sometimes he has a regular mania for bringing out the deepest and pettiest of these [unpleasant, nervous] experiences—things a reasonable man does not trouble himself about or even want to know about, for the simple reason that he would not like to tell them to anyone else [. . .] There will always be men who are justified in this interest in themselves, this detailed observation of their own emotions, poets who can express with clarity and beauty their privileged inner life, and thereby enrich the emotional world of other people. But we are only simple businessmen [. . .] oh, what the devil, we should just sit down and produce something like our forefathers did.

Part 5, chapter 2, p. 207

Though Mann shows Tom to be wrong in supposing these poetic tendencies to be amenable to self-control, he does endorse the notion that poets are a special type of person with a privileged world of feeling.

The novella *Tonio Kröger*, written in 1903, two years after *Buddenbrooks*, investigates this privileged type. Whereas Hanno's emerging, isolating sensibility seemed bewildered and inferior, Tonio Kröger's is set upon a pedestal. He is also the son of a North German merchant (as was Mann) whose business is on the decline, and the problems he faces are similar to Hanno's, in other words, the incapacity for normal, practical, healthy life and the burden of longing which is also a joy; but the problematic tension is eclipsed by the glamour of the artist. Tonio Kröger is a self-assured, famous writer who is trying to define himself (as an artist, of course) vis-à-vis the ordinary man, and an irritating narcissism arises from Mann's treatment of this theme.

This is a common pitfall in the Romanticist's presentation of the art/life opposition. His commitment to art emerges as pride and arrogance. First the artist feels dissatisfied with ordinary life, and the imagination, which absorbs the energy and interest normally addressed to life, struggles confusedly to realise itself. When the artist discovers that creative work can satisfy his imagination and, at the same time, give him an esteemed position in the ordinary world, he is amazed to see what he thought to be a defeat turn out to be a triumph. When his creative impulses were incipient he could only be judged according to ordinary criteria, and he half believed the world's assessment of him as inadequate. When he impresses the world with his creative achievement, he too believes in the goodness of his success, and is angry at the past humiliations. He has succeeded in face of discouragement and disdain; his success is his alone, and he wishes to define the solitary path as a superior one.

Tonio Kröger pretends to explore the difficulties of being an artist while it actually promotes the glamour of those difficulties. Kröger's insistence that it is impossible for the artist not to envy the ordinary man is—it is clear from the novella itself—a great deal of nonsense. Kröger has two very different conceptions of the commonplace (or non-artistic) person, and there is no attempt to reconcile them. First, there is the blond, laughter-loving, blithe, elegant, athletic person. It is under this description of 'ordinary person' that Kröger claims to envy him; but since this type of person is rather stupid—as one must be, Kröger reflects, in order to be lovable—and since Mann so heavily underlines the artist's intelligence and profundity, the envy, to be convincing, needs more explanation than Mann offers.

The theme of the artist's envy, though subject to narcissistic pitfalls, can be done well. Henry James, for example, in *The Lesson of the Master* makes the point that Mann begins to make in *Tonio Kröger*. The life James's artists admire and which threatens their art is seen in a young woman and in 'the life she embodied, the young purity and richness of which appeared to imply that real success was to resemble *that*, to bloom, to present the perfection of a fine type, not to have hammered out headachy fancies with bent back at an ink-stained table'. [4] It is this kind of admiration that Kröger believes he feels, but neither he nor Mann have James's real respect for this fine type. For the superficial description of commonplace loveliness and health is eclipsed by the second conception of the common man who is ignorant of the artist's excellence. As a boy Kröger keeps a notebook of verse which is discovered by his schoolmates and schoolmasters who laugh at such nonsense: 'Consul Kröger's son found their attitude both cheap and silly, and despised his schoolmates and masters as well, and in his turn (with extraordinary penetration) saw through and disliked their personal weaknesses and bad breeding' (p. 132). [5] As an established writer Kröger despises common people because they think that an artist's work is merely another social asset; he grudges their insensitivity to the artist's struggle against society. Moreover, it seems that the ordinary person has no capacity for self-expression other than sentimental outpourings. On the ship which is taking him to Denmark, Kröger meets a red-haired, freckled-face— in short, very common—man who tries to describe his admiration for the night sky, but the effect is totally banal. Indeed, rather than the envy and love for the common man which allegedly inspires Kröger's work, we see, primarily, the artist's superiority.

Tonio Kröger's detachment from life stems not only from the artist's inability to cope with normal demands—an inability shared by Hanno—but also from his need, as an artist, to be unimpeded by emotion or commitment. In subsequent works, specifically in *Death in Venice*, Mann develops this theme with power, subtlety and originality, but here he merely states Romantic platitudes. First, detachment is recommended because involvement in the artist's subject-matter prevents him from controlling his expression. A fellow writer tells Kröger that he cannot work in the spring because the season fills him with varied, irrelevant sensations which, when used in his art, turn out to be trash. Kröger himself, during a storm at sea, tries to compose a poem, but his heart is too full of feeling for anything good to come of the effort. This analysis of creative impasse, however, is unsatisfactory. At best it gestures towards a critical objection to the work itself, indicating a onesidedness or sentimentality in the work. There are too many counterexamples of artists being in love with their work or inspired by love or moved to madness or delight by the power of their imaginations to allow weight to the belief that this kind of detachment is, in general, an artistic necessity.

Secondly, a more extreme detachment is recommended for the artist. Good art, Tonio Kröger concludes—and Mann seems to endorse his conclusion—can only come from a bad life; one must die to life to be utterly a creator. But what is this bad life Kröger must lead? Is it merely loneliness and emotionlessness? In that case, how can he account for the irritations and icy ecstasies of the artist's nervous system, of the sensual and intellectual excesses from which his health suffers but which strengthen his art? Even if he pursues these adventures, as Mann says, with a dead heart, he is not avoiding life. Here again the novella states but does not consistently develop its theme.

Tonio Kröger presents the isolation of the artist as an anguish to be enjoyed. At sixteen Kröger retreats from a dancing class where he, as a child of the imagination, does not belong. He cannot achieve the life elegance represented by the dance, nor can he find acceptance from the blond, blue-eyed, laughter-loving children in the class. He gazes at a window, too absorbed in his inward vision to notice that the blind is drawn. He wonders why he is different from other people, and why he must suffer.

To feel stirring within you the wonderful and melancholy play of
strange forces and to be aware that those others you yearn for and
blithely inaccessible to all that moves you—what pain that is! And
yet. He stood there alone and aloof [. . .] But yet he was happy.
For he lived. His heart was full [. . .]

p. 144

Though Mann is in general quick to point out the indulgences to
which the Romanticist is prone, he is not critical of this melancholy,
which is really only a combination of superiority and self-pity. The
novella endorses the division between art and life, for it presents the
artist's alienation in a glamorous light rather than a problematic one.
The artist is set above life, and his envy of the rabble's life-ease is a
fraud. The common, or normal person here, as in *Buddenbrooks*, is
insignificant beside the artist, who, for all his misery and isolation, is
shown to be a privileged and glamorous type.

Throughout his works Mann places the artist in a special position,
but he overcame this early narcissism and achieved both profoundly
comic and profoundly tragic realisations of this theme.

The aggrandised position of the central character in the allegorical
novel *Royal Highness* takes over from Kröger's melancholic self-
importance: 'Known by all and yet a stranger, he moves among the
crowd, surrounded by it and yet as though isolated in a void. He walks
alone and on his narrow shoulders carries the burden of his royal
station.'[6] Though this novel is at times affected by a sentimentality similar to that of *Tonio Kröger*, Klaus Heinrich's royal position
actually protects this allegorical representation of the artist from
Kröger's oppressive glamour, for the superiority of the Prince is a
donnée and is not underlined over and over again. Furthermore,
Tonio Kröger's position is here shown to be pathetic and even
grotesque. The person who represents his dictum that the artist must
die to life to be utterly a creator is the poet Klaus Heinrich honours for
a piece extolling the joys of life. The poet, though only thirty-three
years old, is sallow, ill, ugly, reserved and depressed, and though in his
works he uses the first person when he praises life he, as a poet, is
forbidden life's joys. Life, he informs the Prince, is unhygienic—even
normal health is unhygienic, for creativeness arises only from poor
health. But whereas Kröger, in the style of *Sturm und Drang*,
proclaims literature to be not a calling but a curse, the poet in *Royal
Highness* shows Mann's increasing doubts as to the genuine seriousness of the artist, for he says that literature is not a calling but a refuge

from his own inadequacies. Kröger pretended to love life, while Mann himself could portray life only as superficial and banal; Klaus Heinrich's poet is grateful to literature for providing him with an excuse to withdraw from life.

There are several points of similarity between the poet and his Prince. Klaus Heinrich's prospective father-in-law complains that the Prince has no real profession, that his life consists only of ceremonies, and the Prince, in turn, asks the poet what his profession is, for he cannot understand how a person's life-work can be poetry. Both, also, are forbidden ordinary life. The Prince, however, has a naïve and eager interest in the normal and the commonplace. He would be delighted to participate in life, but the barrier is set up by commonplace people who need to sustain the image royalty presents to them.

Art as represented allegorically by Klaus Heinrich does not stem from a privileged inner life; art is not expression and profundity and anguish; it is studied appearances; it is elegance and beauty. In the same year *Royal Highness* was published (1909) Mann was writing the first part of *Felix Krull* in which art as appearance is shown to be art as illusion and deception. In both works people's need for lovely images and their need to be deceived as to the prosaic truth lying behind these images is investigated. As a child the Prince learns that the emotional life of royal people is important only as a public display. He wonders whether his mother truly loves him, and it is not pure irony on Mann's part—it is not irony of the type that would pertain to an ordinary woman of society—when the Prince concludes that she does love him, when she has time, though the loveliest expression of her love is reserved for diplay, to gladden people's hearts with the sight of royal-maternal affection. Lovely images fulfil an important human need and should therefore not be dismissed as vain or empty. It is royalty's proper duty to embody the ideals of the people, so that when they applaud the Prince they are actually applauding themselves or, rather, the realisation of their own imaginations. In response to the poetic image he presents to them, they offer to him only select images of themselves. Part of the people's love for the Prince stems from the image he gives them of themselves. Art as illusion is necessary for good morale.

It is a peculiarity of Mann's treatment of the art/life opposition that when he presents art as illusion he acknowledges the artist's dependence upon life, but that when he presents artists such as Kröger, Aschenbach and Leverkühn, whose art concerns psychological and spiritual truths, the opposition seems nearly complete. Felix Krull's capacity for deception—that is, his art of illusion—depends upon very careful observation of life; and Klaus Heinrich, who presents a more favourable view of the ultimate value of image, seeks rejuvenation and stimulus from the real world. The calculated appearances of which his life consists should not be merely artificial; as in the case of Felix Krull, the effectiveness of the Prince's image depends upon its representation of a higher truth. In *Felix Krull* the notion of a higher truth is sheer irony, for it is the truth of the imagination, which longs to be deceived; but in *Royal Highness* the value of this truth is endorsed. To prevent the royal position from stagnation and artificiality Klaus Heinrich marries a woman of a foreign, exacting nature, whose modern intelligence and enterprise revive the inbred nation.

To win this woman Klaus Heinrich must convince her that he is not a mere actor, that his studied appearance has its source in human feeling and need. The Prince's courtship of Imma is unique in Mann's work, for here the need of personal connection forces a reconciliation between art and life, and this reconciliation does not defeat either art or life but is advantageous to them both. Much of the material is based upon Mann's own courtship of his wife. Some of Klaus Heinrich's letters are virtual copies of Mann's letters to Katia, and there is real warmth and sensitivity and simple, human longing in the scenes with the Prince and Imma and her father. The reconciliation between the art of royal image and the reality of humanity, however, is extremely simplistic. When the Prince kneels before Imma he presents her with two things: his deformed hand, the one impediment to a calling that demands a perfect appearance, and a rose from the Old Castle grounds which produces magnificent-looking but musty-smelling flowers. Vulnerable humanity and royal magnificence and decay thus reach out to life and youth. This unsatisfactory naïveté is mirrored in Mann's description of the effect this marriage has on the country. Imma, a student of mathematics, gives the Prince sufficient instruction to enable him to handle the State's financial problems, and Imma's father becomes such an effective financial adviser that the country comes out of its longstanding depression.

For all its emphasis on rejuvenation and growth, this novel pales beside those works in which the artist is trapped within his own decadence. Imagination which is capable of such easy reconciliation with life, is effete; it lacks the dæmonic magic from which Hanno suffered and which was to be the subject of Mann's later works. The

Prince, as representative of the imagination, is merely charming and too shallow to be interesting. The significant problem in the opposition between art and life stems from the fact that the imagination is not satisfied by pleasing royal ceremonies but by visions inspired by a profound sense of truth, yet which are not to be found in real life. Imagination, in its opposition to life, often seems more profound than life; it craves concentrated and subtle truths about the extreme poles of consciousness, both dæmonic and ecstatic; it loves powerful effects and startling, vivid images which deflect the moderation and compromises necessary to normal life. It is upon this theme of ambiguously balanced value that Mann's own imagination thrived, and thus the simple integration proposed in *Royal Highness* is a side-step rather than a final resolution.

3 The Death Enchantment

My passion for the Wagnerian enchantment began with me as soon as I knew of it, and began to make it my own and penetrate it with my understanding. All that I owe to him of enjoyment and instruction, I can never forget: the hours of deep and single bliss in the midst of theatre crowds, hours of nervous and intellectual transport and rapture, of insights of great and moving import such as only his art offers. My zeal is never weary, I am never satiated, with watching, listening, admiring—not, I confess, without misgivings; but the doubts and objections do as little harm to my zeal as did Nietzsche's immortal critique, which has always seemed to me like a panegyric with the wrong label, like another kind of glorification. [1]

Mann's attitude towards Wagner outlines his ambivalent Romanticism. This crafty weaver of spells, as Mann called the composer, was adept in all the arts of insinuation and fascination and was able to wield his magic with a devil's sensuousness. The power of his music is allied to a death wish. The urgent desire heard in his music is strangely inward-looking, and its object is often longing itself. This longing consumes energy, even the energy of passion; its infinity is crushing, and issues in the desire for infinite stasis, which is also death—and this deathly image is presented by music so entrancing that it seems to be the highest good. The power of the music makes life look impoverished; its effect is hypnotic, and it paralyses the ordinary will to live. Fulfilment seems to lie not in active life, but in release from life's limitations and in glorification of measureless, ever-intensifying longing.

The concept of music as an expression of the sensuous and dæmonic can be derived from composers other than Wagner. Kierkegaard, in *Either, Or*, defined music as the immediate and dæmonic expression of sensuousness, yet Mozart was the centre of his musical world. He saw *Don Giovanni* as the supreme opera—or what he calls the perfect, classic opera—because its form and content are identical; that is, the realisation of its subject is a realisation of music's essential nature. *Don Giovanni* is the expression of the dæmonic determined as the sensuous; the Don himself is absolutely musical—he seduces with the dæmonic power of sensuousness.

The sensuous quality of Mozart's opera, however, is importantly different from that of Wagner's music. The compulsion of the Don's unending desire stems from vitality, and a passionate need to exert himself upon the world. However desperate and destructive the Don may be, he represents the joy of life. As Kierkegaard says, he represents energy, storm, impatience and passion in all their lyrical quality. It is the blind urgency and quickness of his desire which makes it dæmonic. The Don masters all distractions and delights in chance meetings and obstacles; his darting attentions are at odds with the earnest single-mindedness of Wagnerian characters. The yearning heard in the works of the Romantic composer is a yearning which seems to move on and on, but in one direction; it is a yearning for something beyond the world rather than, as in the case of the Don, a yearning for the whole world. Wagner's mastery of elemental urge and image is coupled with a desire for release from elemental forces— and, as in Schopenhauer's metaphysics, there is in his music an identification of release from life with submergence in the elemental core of life. Mann was fascinated by this ambiguity, and it is this ambiguity upon which Nietzsche's critique focused.

Nietzsche's early work, *The Birth of Tragedy from the Spirit of Music*, is dedicated to Richard Wagner. In this essay he discusses the origins of Greek tragedy and says that the tragic chorus, which at one time constituted the total drama, has its source in music. It is the expression of the inchoate will and it reveals energy and elemental instinct as the most profound aspect of life. This, of course, is the Dionysian world of pain and contradictory impulses and tormented ecstasy as opposed to the Apollonian world of beautiful images and graceful proportion, which has its source in dream and the ideal rather than in music. The chorus represented a barbaric force which is eternal, and unchanged by civilising influences. Modern scientific optimism, the belief that human nature is subject to infinite improvement, however, denies the primeval forces upon which tragedy is based. The complementary redeeming image, the Apollonian image, is also denied, for such redemption can be conceived only as compensation for life's implacable horror.

Neither element of tragedy, in light of the modern belief in improvement and happiness, has been realised for some time; but,

Nietzsche declares, Richard Wagner has once again plumbed the Dionysian depths. It would be impossible, he says in this early essay, for a musical person to listen to the third act of *Tristan und Isolde* as a purely symphonic movement—without, that is, the modifying specifications of character and situation—and not expire beneath the clear and terrible presentation of the world Will.

At the time of writing this essay Nietzsche believed vitality to be compatible with, even connected to, immeasurable longing, but fourteen years later he added a foreword to *The Birth of Tragedy* in which he expresses regret for his youthful enthusiasm. He now describes the music as pure Romanticism, with the double effect of a narcotic that both intoxicates and spreads a fog. This Romanticism is a form of disease, a suffocation, a religious absurdity. This last accusation was directed specifically against *Parsifal*, the opera which made Nietzsche's disillusion with the composer final. This religious opera offered proof to him of the composer's decadence, which previously he had mistaken for strength. Nietzsche no longer sees the music as plumbing the deepest sources of life; he sees it as the work of an overexcited sensibility that requires stronger and stronger stimuli. Wagner knows how to excite weary nerves, and he therefore attracts the exhausted and the decadent. What had once seemed to Nietzsche a resurgence of life, is now understood as a safeguard of the decrepit, the false, the impoverished, the nihilistic. Wagner makes eyes at master morality—that is, at the importance of the noble, free spirit— but then mouths the contradictory doctrine, the doctrine of the need for redemption. Nietzsche turns aside from his admiration of the Apollonian vision as a means of redeeming pain. He now sees his hero as the man who can accept and even embrace life's awfulness for all eternity, without hope or even longing for redemption. The only relief such a hero has is in life-exultation and in his own strength. Wagner's music cannot provide this, the only true and honest relief, for it is sluggish and lacks divine dance rhythms. Dionysian art emerges from a overfull vitality, but Wagner appeals to those who are life-impoverished and who demand from art either calm soothing ease on the one hand, or frenzy, convulsion and anaesthesia on the other.

There is indeed something incontrovertible in the claim that Wagner's music presents a powerful sense of absence. Longing is central to many of his operas, and this longing is different from ordinary desire, which is the desire to do something or to obtain something. Normally, desire involves the will to some action—

certainly Don Giovanni's desire is bound up with the need to act and to assert himself. The desire mapped out in *Tristan und Isolde*, however, is suspended in a continuously intensifying sensuousness for which no fulfilment seems possible or even desirable. The yearning is gigantic and far surpasses the characters' desire for one another—a desire which could possibly be fulfilled. Of course Don Giovanni's desire can never be fulfilled, but only in the sense that it will always be renewed. The insatiability of his desire is based upon the fact that his present, particular desire will be satisfied, forgotten and then immediately renewed as it finds some other female object. The longing of Tristan and Isolde, however, does not have the relief either of momentary satisfaction or distraction. Their desire is a glorification of passion, and its satisfaction would be its negation, not its fulfilment. The increasing intensity of the longing becomes a desire for death— not simply because the exquisite longing is too great a burden, but because death alone, in the Romantic image of death, can fulfil immeasurable desire by mystically suspending and preserving it. Tristan says that he is all love, that this love—which is his self—is eternal, and therefore he is eternal; but the sense in which he is eternal is the sense in which he is immortal in death. His eternal love has taken over his self; he has no interests or desires apart from this love, and therefore his desire is not to possess the individual, changing, human Isolde; his desire is to sustain and freeze this longing. The kingdom of his love is the night, safe from the prosaic tasks of the day. His desire demands the timelessness and changelessness of death—of, that is, the Romantic notion of death, according to which death provides the intensity and perfection which life denies.

Wagner wrote to Mathilde Wesendonk: 'Often I look with yearning towards the land of Nirvana. But Nirvana soon becomes *Tristan* again'. Indeed, *Tristan und Isolde* is open to a nihilistic interpretation for it presents fulfilment as the extinction of the self. The opera has an affinity to Schopenhauer's metaphysics, though, as a love story and a glorification of love, satisfaction is not found in suppression of the characters' wills. To Schopenhauer love was one of the stronger and baser forms of Will. Though love might overpower the will to individual life, this would only be an example of one will overpowering another; love is essentially desire and therefore it is essentially Will. The death Isolde joyfully embraces is not, according to Schopenhauer's views, annihilation, for in dying she merges with ever-surging, ever-striving energy. She is participating in, not suppressing, her will; her individual will rejoins the primal Will and rejoices in its eternal power. Nevertheless, the image in the opera of the elemental core of life as Will is Schopenhauerian, as is the notion of Will as endless longing and of death as reunion with the universal Will. Fulfilment, in the opera, comes not through an end of longing but through an eternal intensification of longing; both spiritual and sensual fulfilment are found in death.

The love–death ecstasy in *Tristan und Isolde* is only one of several examples of Wagner's presentation of death as an apparent good. The two thunderous C major chords of Siegfried's funeral march present the tragedy of the hero's death as a savage triumph, and Brünnhilde leaps upon the funeral pyre with exultation, believing that in death the love life denied her will be found. And, closely associated with the Nirvana longing, is the shimmering suspension of energy and emotion, a brilliant consolidation of intensity and stasis, of yearning which is both heightened and satisfied by a beautiful image—such as the dying Siegfried's address to Brünnhilde, or Parsifal's vision of the meadow on Good Friday. Then, there are innumerable examples of a phrase of unbearable sadness or tenderness which is also unbearably beautiful, so that the sense of absence expressed by the music seems valuable because of its beauty—such as the motive of Wotan's farewell or Brünnhilde's pleading or the transformation and crescendo of the Freya motive as Siegfried kisses the sleeping Brünnhilde. None of these examples indicates a death wish peculiar to Wagner alone. The last type is exhibited by most great composers. Schubert's mastery of mingling sadness and beauty, and his presentation of the desirability of stasis and extinction, made him the perfect representative of Romanticism's enchanting song of death in *The Magic Mountain*. But the preponderance and power of the death wish in Wagner, the way it is glorified and energised, explain Mann's identification of the composer with the death enchantment.

Mann said that Wagner has the erotic honey and passion of Schopenhauer without his wisdom. In Wagner there is a full understanding of the destructiveness of the erotic will, but no impulse to suppress or even modify it. In Mann's short story *Tristan*, however, he criticised not the aggressive aspect of the erotic will, but the pain of desire and the longing to be released from everything, from desire itself, which therefore emphasises the Nirvana aspect of the opera; and Mann's criticism becomes a criticism of Schopenhauer more than Wagner.

The story was published in 1902, twenty-two years before *The Magic Mountain*, but combines the same themes of lung disease, music and death and is also set in a mountain sanatorium. In it a writer persuades a woman patient to play the piano while most of the inmates are on a sleigh party. She plays a piano arrangement of the second act of *Tristan und Isolde* which contains the love duet that affirms night as the fundamental reality. 'To him who has looked upon the night of death and known its secret sweets', Mann explains, 'to him death can never be anything but vain, nor can he know a longing save for night, eternal, real, in which he is made one with love'.[2] Mann's characters do not themselves suffer the torture and ecstasy of love, but they are nonetheless overwhelmed by Wagner's glorification of night. Mann's sympathy for their fascination can be seen in his eulogy of sleep in which he more than playfully considers the possibility that the lush green twilights between the active day are one's real place in life.[3] He says that his love for the sea (which in *Tonio Kröger* and *Death in Venice* he associates with imagination) and his love for sleep arise from the same source—from what he calls the Hindu longing, the heavy and sluggish craving for a consummation which is identified with Nirvana or nothingness.

Mann, however, tries to resist the Romantic acceptance of death and dissolution as the highest good. He modifies his praise of sleep by saying that individual existence can be seen as a virtue, as a resolve to concentrate, to limit and to shape, to renounce freedom and infinity and the all-slumbering spaceless and timeless night; existence is a resolve to endure struggle, compulsion, passion and pain. In his moral outlook, then, Mann tries to follow Nietzsche and to resist Schopenhauer's assessment as the highest good as annihilation. Yet Mann's morality never coincided comfortably with his impulses. The night, the Romantic night, the spaceless and timeless chamber of eternity, remained for him the greatest reality and the greatest attraction.

To speak of the death longing in Wagner's music, however, is to use a Romantic term. The Romantic conception of death is not purely negative, and therefore Nietzsche's categorical dismissal of death on behalf of life misses the point. Mann admits the validity of Nietzsche's complaint that the general tone of Wagner's music is heavily permeated with night and death, that it is laden with a sluggish yearning, but he adds that it seems to be wrestling out of the darkness and confusion. The yearning which burdens the soul and draws it into the underworld does not indicate privation but effort, purpose and the possibility of resolution; the seductive Nirvana-like stasis is not mere escapism but a reprieve which quickens the soul; the night world provides strength and energy for life:

> Surely that man is the greatest who keeps faith with and yearns for
> the night, while he performs the mightiest tasks of the day. And so
> it is that I shall love best that work which was born out of 'yearning
> after the glorious holy night', and as it were in spite of itself stands
> today glorious both in slumber and in strength of will—I mean
> Richard Wagner's *Tristan und Isolde.*
>
> *Sleep, Sweet Sleep*[4]

The balance and reciprocity Mann advocates in this essay is never
achieved by his characters, and in his fiction yearning for the 'glorious
holy night' often becomes decadent and destructive rather than life-
enforcing. The story *Tristan* is a burlesque about a writer who
believes imagination should be protected from life. Though the
writer Spinell forces Wagner upon the woman patient who eventually dies from the strain of the music, he blames her death on the
energy and practical-mindedness of the woman's husband and on the
son who is like the father and who drained the mother's strength.
Wagner's opera concentrates for four hours on romantic passion and
presents spiritual transfiguration through passion; without the fury
and conviction of Wagner's vision, the themes are easily caricatured.
Mann suspects the music's intensity, and brings it down to pathetically human size. In doing so, he side-steps the themes of the reality of
passion and passion's mystic aspirations. The theme of the story is the
contemplation of Wagner's opera; it is not the theme of the opera
itself.

'Methodically Constructed', one of the stories in Hermann Broch's
collection *The Guiltless*, also uses the Tristan material (though not
directly, as Mann does when he introduces Wagner's music and uses
the characters' reaction to the music as the main dramatic impetus,
but the *Liebestod* theme and the combined images of night and love
and death clearly relate the story to the opera) with a comic effect; and
Broch's comedy makes a similar point about the superhuman
dimensions of Wagnerian passion. The high school teacher in
'Methodically Constructed' falls in love with his landlady's daughter,
and though at first he is satisfied with the commonplace pleasures of
love, he is soon disturbed by the task of joining his physical love with
a spiritual love. The high-school teacher, with a timid and commonplace respect for method alongside a Romantic view of love,
believes that to honour his love he must continually augment it. To

love his fiancée, and to honour the spiritual aspect of his love, is to strive for some infinitely distant point. His earthbound soul cannot reach this point, and this failure negates the reality of his passion. Only death can free the lovers from the despair of unattainable perfection and universality; only death can demolish the multiplicity and distraction and practicality of their lives; in death the supreme reality of their love would be grasped and held fast. Death, then, is the logical choice of those who want to honour and confirm their love. Usually, however, the aspirations of love are not realised; the commonplace asserts itself against one's spiritual needs, and life goes on.

Broch's treatment of this theme has a warmth and humour which prevent either the commonplace characters or their infinite aspirations from being ridiculous, as Mann's writer Spinell is when, terrified by any display of robust life, he runs away from the Klöterjan baby. Broch's subject is the difficulty of realising one's highest desires—as perceived by the imagination—within life, whereas Mann's subject is the power of the imagination to withhold life. Imagination, as Mann presents it, is totally uninterested in life. The writer in *Tristan* does not wish for a finer, more passionate, more spiritual love for the musical lung patient; he wants her to remain an angelic image in her decaying garden; he wants only the inviolable imaginative vision, not life enhanced or honoured by imagination. In Mann's view the problematic effect of Wagner is not dissatisfaction with life as much as lack of interest in life. Broch's characters are never totally pathetic because they are not locked within one or the other spheres of imagination or life; however comic their earnest, methodical attempts to resolve a Romantic tension, their imaginations honestly seek a life-solution; whereas for Mann the music—the world of imagination—is the ultimate satisfaction. And therein lies the danger. The aesthetic vision becomes the sole reality; life seems contemptible—but the imagination, cut off from life, lacks energy and truth. In *Tristan* imagination is pathetically enclosed and pathetically frightened of life.

Wagner is particularly suited to feature in Mann's theme of the domination of the imagination not only because he is a peculiarly powerful composer but because of the peculiarly demanding world represented in his music. Mozart is not less powerful, but in his operas life and imagination are brought together. The tension between them is investigated with sympathy but with a keen eye to the necessity of resolution. Don Giovanni is the only character who does not adapt to life's limitations and who refuses to compromise. Donna Anna, Elvira and Zerlina, in varying degrees, must reject the appeal of this unyielding force. Figaro and Suzanna are so attractive, and such good survivors, because they quickly grasp the real situation and are able to expose those whose vision is less sure. The reality which inhibits the imagination is part of Mozart's musical world, whereas Wagner's characters are thoroughly imbedded in the imaginative plane. This enclosure is part of the music's strength, part of its Romantic–mythic power, part of its primitive and archaic aspect. Wagner's characters seldom compromise; they are—with the exception of the characters in *Die Meistersinger*—either tragically defeated or blissfully triumphant. Compare, for example, the impossibility of Brünnhilde forgiving the living Siegfried for his infidelity with the Countess's forgiveness of her husband. Compare, too, the fluidity and quickness of the emotions of Mozart's characters with the earnest concentration and intensity of the emotions of Wagner's characters. Wagner throws one into a world formed by the deepest, most demanding and recalcitrant impulses. Within this world these impulses seem more real than the life that would mould or thwart them, for the music presents a pre-social mentality, a mentality which seeks its own logic and its own proportions. Emotion becomes gigantic, and because every impulse is unyielding, the clashes are cataclysmic. The dramas, especially the drama of *Der Ring des Nibelungen*, seem to be enacted according to the laws of the psyche alone; the drama is governed by inner forces, and this gives it a peculiar intensity and necessity.[5] The psychological truths revealed in these dramas are often left behind in Mann's investigations of the music's problematic effects. The power and enormity of the emotions are taken out of context and thus made to seem far more amoral and indulgent than they actually are in the operas.

Hermann Broch presented the vision of a mystical transfiguration of love as a vision arising from the desire to unite the sensual and the spiritual. He placed these mystical aspirations amid the ordinary human comedy where aspirations are often thwarted by one's own mediocre nature. Mann saw the mystical vision arising from an inherent longing for death rather than as an extension of human emotion; and he treated the vision ironically by showing its failure to redeem life in any way. In neither case, however, is the validity of the Wagnerian vision itself denied, whereas Nietzsche saw the vision itself as a fraud—not because life fails to come up to the standards set by this Romantic image or because the power of the image depletes life, but because as an imaginative image it is worthless. Nietzsche claimed that one need only strip Wagner's characters of their heroic skins to make them indistinguishable from Madame Bovary. That is to say, the characters are motivated by sentimentality and boredom rather than by the necessity of full-blooded passion. According to Nietzsche the Wagnerian world is not only unreal in the way Broch and Mann admit, but is also unable to satisfy a truly vivid imagination. Wagnerian emotions arise from the languors of an empty soul; their self-importance stems from selfishness and pettiness rather than from a true, passionate strength.

Though Nietzsche's estimation of Wagner's characters is straight-forwardly wrong, and though Mann never was in doubt as to the incorrectness of this judgement, he saw that certain Wagnerian characteristics could become, when taken from the opera house and brought into life, not passion and mystic sensuousness but lethargy, indulgence and selfishness. In an early story, *The Blood of the Walsungs* (1905), the world of Wagner and that of the soul-impoverished bourgeoisie come together in a way that might seem to support Nietzsche's evaluation of the Wagnerian love-affair. The tale opens with a description of middle class comforts, similar to those described in the opening of *Buddenbrooks*; but here luxury is not the fruit of decent labour; it is a setting for idleness and indulgence. The heavily panelled, heavily carpeted and curtained house of the Aarenhold family does not exhibit the Buddenbrooks' complacency and practicality; rather, it exhibits wealth employed by aesthetic sensi-bilities. It is therefore a setting for decadence and lassitude, with an additional element of savagery, heard in the gong which proclaims the lunch hour and which makes a sound out of all proportion to its use—just as Nietzsche thought the gigantic scale of Wagner's works to be out of all proportion to his message and his talent. In this tale the domestic atmosphere is perfectly blended with the debilitating aspect of the Wagnerian atmosphere; but, despite its title, and despite the names of Siegmund and Sieglinde chosen for the bourgeois twins, and despite the description of the first act of *Die Walküre*, this tale cannot be taken as a comment on Wagner's works themselves because it is about a kind of aestheticism combined with a lack of creativeness and a lack of passion:

> They sat in splendour and security, but their words rang sharp, as though sharpness, hardness, alertness and pitiless clarity were demanded of them as survival values. Their highest praise was a

grudging acceptance, their criticism was ruthless; it snatched the weapons from one's hand, it paralysed enthusiasm, made it a laughing stock. [6]

Aestheticism here is not compelling imagination but critical disdain. Mann says that the twins care only for achievement and power, but this is only a careless flourish upon the cruel aestheticism he is trying to present, for the twins are in fact disdainful of achievement as well as effort and intention, and show no interest in power. Their aestheticism is sheer idleness, elegance and arrogance. There is no ironic indication that their decadent sensibilities actually contain riches of the spirit; their decadence is simply a dead end. They suffer nothing of Hanno's burden of longing—which Hanno found expressed in *Lohengrin*—for their disdain for the world is complete, and there is nothing, either on the practical or spiritual plane, to desire. The twins' separation from life is put into effect not by imaginatively conceived mystical longings, but by preoccupation with the elegant accoutrements of life, which give them no time for life itself. From this idleness and emptiness, grows a distorted, aesthetically biased morality.

Nietzsche would have been delighted by this burlesque on the Wälsung twins. The bourgeois (and possibly Jewish) Siegmund and Sieglinde make love after a performance of *Die Walküre*. Their lovemaking is a reaction, in part, to the love enacted on the stage by their namesakes, but just as their Jewish race offers a travesty on the way people in Germany were at that time interpreting Wagner's Wälsung race, so, too, their their lovemaking is a travesty of Wagnerian passion:

> [. . .] they loved one another with all the sweetness of the senses, each for the other's spoiled and costly well-being and delicious fragrance. They breathed it in, this fragrance, with languid and voluptuous abandon, like self-centred invalids, consoling themselves for the loss of hope. [7]

Their love is narcissistic and sensual, as is the love of the Wälsung twins, but it is completely devoid of the rapturous longing and shattering fulfilment. The Aarenhold twins' love is a counterpart of Wagner's love music bereft of emotion; it is Wagner ironically reduced to the effete sensibility of a certain type of Wagnerian. The twins' craving for art's grandeur becomes, in their lives, petty extravagance; the primitive or archaic element in Wagner's music becomes, in their lives, childishness and selfishness. Siegmund has no understanding of the substance of Wagner's passionate vision. He feels his own limitation as he leans towards the stage:

> Pain gnawed and burned in Siegmund's breast, a drawing anguish that was somehow sweet, a straining—in what direction, for what? It was all so dark, so shamefully unclear! Two thoughts, two words he had: creation, passion. His temples glowed and throbbed, and it came upon him as in a yearning vision that creation was born of passion and reshaped anew as passion.[8]

Siegmund cannot sustain this insight. The substance of his life is idleness and luxury; the longing the music arouses cannot be creative and results only in a casual incestuous episode. This story is a criticism of the use to which a decadent sensibility puts Wagner's music; it is not a comment on the music itself.

The lack of identification in this tale between the effect Wagner has on the twins and a proper understanding of the music is consistent with Mann's continual refusal to blame Wagner for the use to which the National Socialists put his music. Mann sees Wagner as an artist who speaks with the voice of the German people: the folk tale sources of his music, its primitive emotional poetry, its tremendous sensual appeal and Romanticism and popularity make it representative of the German folk. But this nationalism is not destructive; the operas characterise and express the German soul; they do not glorify it at the expense of other nations; they do not advocate German aggression. Whenever Wagner makes a specific reference to Germany's greatness, as in Hans Sachs' final speech in *Die Meistersinger*, it is clear how apolitical are his interests; to Wagner, the German state is non-essential—the greatest value is seen in German art, which will survive the State's inevitable decline.

Mann does not hold Wagner responsible for the destructive uses to which he was put, yet his sympathy with the composer is limited in a way that makes him focus primarily on the deathward movement of the music. The Romantic metaphor of death longing has connections with the literal meaning of wanting to die, but it would be misleading to identify the literal meaning with the Romantic metaphor. Many Romanticists actually find death attractive but they find it attractive, usually, because the notion of death is given content in addition to— or even in opposition to—its literal meaning as cessation of life. The deathward movement of Wagner's music is due to its archaic aspect and to the boundlessness of the emotions expressed. The gigantic force and intractability of these emotions put a tremendous burden upon the social self, which must regulate and modify impulses. Such a burden creates the life reluctance from which Hanno suffered; but the death he longed for was a death of the social self. This death is seen as a return to deeper, more vital forces than those that can remain intact within the ordinary world. It is expansion and renewal that are sought rather than actual annihilation; yet in the pre-social, archetypal character, these forces have an affinity with dream and night and therefore with death. This primitive vitality resists restraint and thus resists the demands of reality and of practicality. Wagner's appeal to unmodifiable urges stimulates the desire to escape physical and social limitations, and such an escape can be imagined only in death.

Nonetheless, the archaic, urgent emotions and the burden of impulses which continually resist reality's impact are not, in Wagner, merely negative. Their dramatic realisation asserts a human reality; for however problematic the psyche's needs are when confronted with the world's facts, shallowness results from ignoring them. The Romantic 'deathward' movement extends the understanding of the psyche and of its possibilities. Mann, however, concentrated primar- ily upon the negative aspects of this Romantic interest. The desire for Nirvana was for Mann a desire to escape the practical world, and the burdensome longing arose from an inability to direct desire towards the world. Siegmund's fleeting—his merely fleeting—glimpse of the passion which created these dramas indicates Mann's own limitation. Mann could assert, in his essays, that the forces set against common- place, practical control were creative, but he could not, in his fiction, show them to be positive, lasting creative goods.

Death in Venice, one of Mann's finest works, reveals his recalcitrant mistrust of those impulses and emotions which are so vividly presented in Wagner's works. This novella does not discuss Wagner directly, as do *Tristan* and *The Blood of the Walsüngs*, but it presents Mann's attitudes towards death, passion and the debilitating effects of beauty in a way that makes Aschenbach's story similar to one of Wagnerian contagion. The novella reveals the stagnation of Mann's own imagination, yet it treats this impasse so vividly that the negative resolution is transcended by the excellence of the creative presentation.

The story concerns a man who cannot find his way through the maze of sensuality and beauty, who becomes ensnared by a love- fascination that both excites and enervates him. His desires fluctuate among crude sensual longings, tender protectiveness and spiritual cravings. The fluctuation destroys the familiar boundaries of his personality and crushes him with confusion. At the opening of the novella Aschenbach is a respectable, disciplined writer whose forbears were—with the exception of one lively clergyman and a musical grandfather—officers, civil servants and judges. Though he is an artist he retains his forefathers' restraint and regimented lifestyle. This fastidious control is the focal point of his weakness: Aschenbach's impulses have, from childhood, been totally suppressed and, in their neglect, have remained untutored so that when they emerge, they emerge in a thoroughly crude and primitive fashion.

This analysis does not use a specifically Freudian model, for, according to Freud, impulses are always untutored and must always be repressed to some extent, though if they are repressed too severely, they will emerge as a neurotic symptom. The salvation of the civilised personality is achieved by a balance of impulse and control, and, in any person born into any human society, there will be a continuous balance, however precarious or unsatisfactory, between impulse and control. Mann's model of total suppression and then violent release has more in common with Euripide's portrayal of Pentheus's struggle against Dionysus. Here, the man who trusts reason's strength and thus his own self-control is guilty of *hubris*. His punishment is to be torn apart by the Maenads, the representatives of impulse in its crude, orgiastic state. *Death in Venice* does not actually contradict a Freudian model, but the pattern of Aschenbach's decay is fashioned upon the Greek myth.

Aschenbach's byword is 'hold-fast'. The type of hero he favours in his writing is one who shows forbearance in the face of fate, or who remains constant under torture. In short, he is interested in heroism born of weakness. He believes that every conspiciously great achievement has resulted from adverse circumstances—from pain, poverty, physical weakness, vice, passion. This view of greatness is similar to that of Nietzsche, who carried the point further by suggesting that since adversity bred greatness, adversity should be propagated. Aschenbach, however, does not so vigorously deny a humanist morality. In highly unNietzschean fashion he bypasses those investigations of human nature which might deprive him of his firm moral line. Since his own impulses and emotions are suppressed, he knows nothing of those creative—destructive energies which blur distinctions between good and evil. Indeed, his safe, sober respectability has little contact with the suffering, vice and passion of which he writes in a fine classical style and which is reproduced in school textbooks. Aschenbach's interest in formal perfection is part of his denial of the vast undergrowth of life; and, at the same time, it makes him particularly susceptible to this amoral, violent undergrowth. Classical form, according to Mann, has two aspects: it reveals a moral strength because it is the result of discipline, but it reveals an immoral tendency in its esteem for beauty—for beauty concerns form and elegance alone; it cares nothing of either good or evil. The artist might turn away from the dark, ugly side of nature and devote himself to beauty and hope thereby to discover a spiritual, sublime image; but beauty, even if it eventually leads to the spiritual, first acts upon the senses. This makes beauty perilous, and for this reason imagination itself is wanton. For imagination is not affected by reason, morality or practicality; it is affected by beauty and good form. Aschenbach's respect for good form (or sensuous manifestation) combined with his detachment (that is, his proud denial of his uncivilised impulses) leads directly to the abyss of irrationality and passion; since beauty appeals to the senses, the detached rationality cannot regulate the impulses thereby aroused, and the impulses follow a rabid, extravagant course.

This is the theoretical outline of the novella. There is, however, little content given to the divine which the artist allegedly tries to approach through beauty or to the special relation beauty might, in the best of circumstances, have with the divine. The quasi-Platonic model (in the *Symposium* love is seen as a link between the sensible world and the world of Forms; it prompts the soul to recapture the vision of the ideal world) is used as an unargued premise. The spiritual is simply posited as the opposite of sensuous fascination, and therefore the assertion that Aschenbach's love for Tadzio is spiritual yearning gone wrong carries no conviction. Indeed, it is impossible to believe, from the very beginning of the tale, that Aschenbach's desires are anything other than sensual. In any great love passion, both sensual and spiritual, will be mingled to the point at which the distinction between them is invidious; but Aschenbach's yearning is always degrading. Moreover, all the seductive arguments in the novella are on the side of decadence and extravagance. The foul-smelling lagoon of Venice whose air Aschenbach inhales with tender, deep, almost painfully sweet draughts, the hateful, insinuating sultriness of the narrow streets in whose stagnant air cigarette smoke remains suspended, the faintly rotten scent of the sea breeze and the sirocco which excites and enervates at once—these command the poetic sympathy of the novella.

A craving for this decay initially motivates Aschenbach, and the longing he suffers is different from anything in Wagner. For decadent though Wagner's sensuousness may at times appear in its enormity and egoism, his characters' desires, even as they emerge from the archaic bed of impulse, are never directed towards the crude and the primitive. The vision which eventually leads Aschenbach to Venice, however, is a regression to the wild and cruel aspects of the primitive. The vision seems to the writer like a 'most surprising widening of the inward barriers' but these barriers are widened only in the sense of being lowered; their profundity is purely regressive:

> Desire projected itself visually: his fancy, not quite lulled since morning, imagined the marvels of the manifold earth. He saw. He beheld a landscape, a tropical marshland, beneath a reeking sky, steaming, monstrous, rank—a kind of primeval wilderness-world of islands, morasses, and alluvial channels. Hairy palm-trunks rose near and far out of the lush brakes of fern, out of bottoms of crass vegetation, fat, swollen, thick with incredible bloom. There were trees, misshapen as in a dream,.that dropped their naked roots straight through the air into the ground or into the water that was stagnant and shadowy and glassy-green, where mammouth milk-white blossoms floated, and strange high-shouldered birds with curious bills stood gazing sidewise without sound or stir. Among the knotted joints of a bamboo thicket the eyes of a crouching tiger gleamed—and he felt his heart throb with terror, yet with a longing inexplicable.[9]

The compelling realism of this hallucination is ironic and, alongside the constant shift from perception to imagination, enforces the uncanny atmosphere in which decay is more vivid than anything else. The precise detail in which the red-haired, snub-nose man is described is also ironic; as he appears in the portico of the cemetery he allegedly calls Aschenbach back to reality—whereas the red-haired man, in fact, is anything but ordinary reality. He reappears in various guises, at various points in the novella, as a messenger of decay. Similar detail of commonplace occurrences—Aschenbach's smarting eyes the morning he leaves for Venice, the nauseous sensation in his stomach as the boat pushes away from port, the seductively comfortable seat of the gondola, the mincing, hate-filled courtesy of the people in the tourist trade—places them alongside Aschenbach's imaginary visions, so that the balance between imagination and perception is totally destroyed. The often overripe virtuosity of the writing is itself an investigation of the imagination from which the fascination with the overripe springs; there is no stable point from which to judge and resist imagination's seduction.

The sea, in its eternal, unorganised simplicity and vastness, is a symbol of the imagination. When Aschenbach first catches sight of Tadzio, the boy is like a figure rising up from the sea, and it is to the sea that Tadzio points while, dying, Aschenbach observes him for the last time. The immensity of expectation, the rich vastness which the sea, as imagination, represents is, however, merely negative. It is release from the degrading tension of intellect and will. It is salvation for the imagination which is confused and made crude by its receptivity to beauty; but the salvation it offers is only death. There can be no higher resolution, for imagination is an impasse of the soul; its receptivity to beauty leads to degradation.

The smile Tadzio offers the writer in response to his joy at seeing the boy again is over-powerful; its effect is similar to that of Wagner's music in its enervating intoxication. It leads to a thoroughly undisciplined emotional outpouring. Aschenbach whispers 'the hackneyed phrase of loving and longing—impossible in the circumstances, absurd, abject, ridiculous enough yet sacred too, and not unworthy of honour even here: "I love you!"' [10] Yet in contrast, the enthralment of Wagner's music has a freshness and expectancy; even the Flower Maidens' seductive song is innocent in comparison to Tadzio's semi-intentional coquetry. The worthiness of this outburst is about equal to Alberich's pursuit of the Rhinemaidens. When Wagner focuses upon passion there is obviously a possibility of goodness and tenderness which Aschenbach's attraction to Tadzio lacks. Aschenbach's passion is stagnant partly because it is isolated, as emotion in Mann's work tends to be. Even Kundry's attempted seduction of Parsifal, however, a seduction which means to be destructive, involves a human exchange, a confrontation of emotion and need that deepens the understanding of both characters; but between Tadzio and Aschenbach only smiles and glances are exchanged. Any deeper, more personal communication, Mann suggests, would break the enchantment. His attraction, then, does not have the Wagnerian conviction which denies the daylight world; rather, Aschenbach knows the weakness of his passion and therefore hides it from the world. Only in isolation and in fear of normality can his 'love' survive. Mann does not present a passion which happens to go wrong; he presents a passion which can exist only if it does go wrong.

Aschenbach's debilitating infatuation is closely connected to his meagre store of energy. Mann continually points to the writer's fragile resources—how his strength must be absorbed from outside sources and then put to some special purpose: he sacrifices to his art, in two or three hours of almost religious fervour, the strength he assembles from sleep. His discipline is a necessity, for it is a means of gathering up his meagre capacities and, at the same time, a way of making sure he uses up all his energy, so he has none left to corrupt him. Aschenbach exhibits none of the natural vigour or the joy of activity which characterises someone whose energy is a healthy part of his self. His inability to maintain a relaxed flow of energy is essential to the detachment which eventually leads to his destruction. When he does not release all his energy in his writing, he has no other outlet. The strength that flows into him from the sun and sea and idleness erupts in emotional intoxication; but this is an inward, stagnant intoxication. The energy not released in his art becomes an attack upon his soul.

Passion, as presented in Mann's works, is passive; that is, it is not directed toward the attainment of its object. Its action is to degrade the person who suffers the passion; passion's object remains almost incidental. Mann fails to appreciate the positive aspect of Tristan and Isolde's yearning for night because he fails to see passion as union; he sees passion as an emotion that isolates rather than extends the individual. Moreover, this isolation viciously enforces itself, so that not only does passion make its subject turn aside from society, it also makes its subject seek to destroy society: 'Passion is like a crime: it does not thrive on the established order and the common round; it welcomes every blow dealt the bourgeois structure, every weakening of the social fabric, because it therein feels a sure hope for its own advantage'.[11] Aschenbach would happily see all Venice destroyed by the disease, for a death-ridden city would provide a fine setting for the enactment of his lewd fantasies. When he discovers the severity of the plague he is 'feverishly excited, triumphant in possession of the truth at last, but with a sickening taste in his mouth and a fantastic horror at his heart'.[12] This self-knowledge is abhorrent to him, and he knows that this recklessness presents a danger to his own self as well as to others. The primitive and destructive landscape of his initial vision has been realised in his passion for Tadzio, and this landscape, too, is the cause of the disease; for the cholera has come from the 'hot moist swamps of the Ganges, where it bred in the mephitic air of that primaeval island-jungle, among whose bamboo thickets the tiger crouched . . .'.[13]

Tristan and Isolde's love also destroys the social fabric, in the sense that their love disregards social order; but such destruction is not the point of their passion, as it is the point of Aschenbach's passion. The purpose of the opera characters' passion is a mystical union, a consummation of a love that brings all longing—sensual and spiritual—together. The harm they do is through neglect of everything other than their passion; and even when their society kills them for this neglect, they assert passion's reality above the reality of death. Mann's view of a passion that disregards all else is of a will to destroy all else. Death, then, is the mitigation of violence. Tristan and Isolde pass into death through an assertion of their vision; their death forces home the Romantic metaphor of death as spiritual realisation, infinite promise and mystical union. Aschenbach's imagination is too confused to make this triumphant leap. As he gazes out to the sea, as Tadzio seems to be hovering before an immensity of richest expectation, there is only the vaguest sense that the tension will be resolved; the only real possibility seems to be that the tension will be dissolved in death.

The archaic undergrowth of human impulse cannot enrich imagination or life because any investigation of this undergrowth will destroy life and mind. Mann's Romanticism is that of the moralist whose principles are as rigidly rational as those of Aschenbach (who deals only with the rational aspects of man) but who is intrigued by the amoral energies which, he half realises, are the sources of imagination and emotion. Aschenbach's favourite hero, the man who achieves strength through weakness and adversity, uses his will only in a highly moral fashion. The blackness of the will which appears in the course of the tale reveals the moralist's frenzied self disgust at the true nature of his will.

The closing sentence reads, 'And before nightfall a shocked and respectful world received news of his decease'.[14] Mann assumes that the public wants to believe in the respectability of the artist, that since the public trusts the artist to reveal human truths the artist himself is expected to be a model of morality. Though the opposite is often the case, though the public delight in the artist's eccentricities and vices and sufferings, Mann here reveals his own expectations of the artist, expectations whose disappointment is often his theme. Mann shows the artist's respectable, spiritual purpose being waylaid by his own imagination; he shows how the discipline necessary to art distorts, through detachment, the artist's human impulses. Here Mann gives content to his dictum that the creator cannot live well. 'Life' is the capacity for self-expression and personal interaction; and the artist's need to give form to the chaos of the human psyche, to tease out the various truths that are packed together in ordinary perception, threatens him with the very chaos he, as an artist, so proudly handles. Indeed, Aschenbach's problem is not simply that he is an artist, but that he is not a great artist. He is therefore unable to look upon all life and to mould its horror creatively, and to balance the horror against the good. The artist's creative material is the mass of sensuousness, impulse and longing which threatens the form and morality he craves. The substance of creation is chaos, and this chaos can destroy the creator.

In this novella the tension between art and life is perfectly realised, but the realisation only shows that the tension, as Mann conceived it, is without resolution. Mann's depiction of imagination's defeat before life, and its inability to handle its own creative material, and its tendency to corrupt its own noble impulses, is an artistic triumph; yet this triumph reveals the defeat of Mann's own imagination, which could not participate in deeper emotional impulses without being hopelessly bewildered, without being able to find a salvation other than annihilation.

4 The Fascination of Disgust

'So sweet was ne'er so fatal', Othello muses in despair as Iago, the anti-spirit, penetrates his soul. This mingling of sweetness and fatality issues in a violent, destructive ecstasy, as it would in the case of a Romanticist; yet Othello's genuine horror at this identification separates Shakespeare's conception from that of the Romanticist. Othello's sensuous vision becomes devoid of tenderness once he is convinced that his senses are grossly misleading, even mocking his spirit. His abuse of Desdemona is a means of rooting out his love for her. He must destroy his emotional world because the anti-spirit Iago has destroyed the harmony between goodness and beauty, between, that is, what satisfies his senses and what satisfies his spirit.

In Romanticism, however, the connections between sweetness and fatality are explored with delight and intrigue. Sometimes this affinity is endorsed because sweetness is more poignant when set beside death, or because only in death will the sweetness—which in life would be short—be preserved. In *The Magic Mountain* Mann avoids this sentimental ploy. In his critical investigation of Romanticism he turns aside from its appreciation of a loveliness that cannot last and turns towards the quick decay and deadliness which are shown to be attractive in their own right. The view that death and disease are lovely things is presented with relentless irony, and their disgusting aspects are continually underlined; but the disgust itself has an irrefutable appeal. Fatality is sweet, and nothing can be other than banal without its aid.

The point and good of life in the Berghof Sanatorium, and the power of its attraction are one with its feverish, decaying atmosphere:

Rendered torpid, as often, by the beer and music, [Hans Castorp] sat with his head to one side and his mouth slightly open, watching the gay, spa-like scene, feeling, not as a disturbing influence, but rather as a heightening of the general singularity, and lending it one mental fillip the more, the fact that all these people were inwardly attacked by nearly resistless decay, and that most of them were feverish.

Chapter 4, p. 112[1]

When Hans Castorp learns that he belongs to this feverish crowd, that he, too, has the disease, the will to corruption—which is the impetus of the entire novel—erupts with a terrible joy:

> For as he lay he would be shaken from deep within by a frantic burst of triumphant laughter, while his heart stood still and suffered something he had never before known, an extravagant joy and hope; then again he grew pale from shock and fear, and it was conscience itself that knocked, in the very throbs of his heart as it pulsed against his ribs.

Chapter 5, p. 184

But conscience (*Gewissens*)—as conscience rather than as fear or habit—can function only upon the belief of some good, and the will to corruption makes the corrupt seem good. Therefore conscience cannot protect him.

In the sanatorium all moral notions are stripped of their practical, resolute, 'Buddenbrook' content. Respect for decay develops its own moral language. The director of the sanatorium speaks of the air on the mountain as being good for disease. In ordinary language this would mean that the air was a good cure for disease, but Hofrat Behrens means that the air speeds up the course of the disease, that the air brings out the symptoms, so that many people who pass for healthy people in the ordinary world below, reveal the disease when they come to the sanatorium. When the Hofrat speaks of some one as a 'good patient' he does not mean that the patient does what is necessary to bring him back to health, but that the patient has a respect for his illness and a talent for exhibiting its symptoms. When the Hofrat congratulates Hans Castorp for doing well, he means to praise him for the way the disease is manifesting itself; he congratulates him not for getting well but for showing the 'normal' symptoms of the disease.

Not only is the Hofrat's notion of good determined by his respect for disease, but, also, his notion of life is derived from the notion of decay. Hans Castorp asks him, 'What is life?' and he replies that it is combustion, a breaking down of chemicals; that it is, in short, decay and dissolution. The Hofrat gloats over this paradox, and though Mann does not endorse this definition, he does see more in it that what it actually is—a shallow play upon words. Indeed, this view of life is tied to Mann's definition of Romanticism as 'the fruit of life, conceived by death, pregnant of dissolution'. Unlike the Hofrat, however, Mann imagines a finer world in which the captivating focus upon decay will be overcome. In this novel the overpowering of the Romantic enchantment involves more than the simple, robust practical nature of first generation Buddenbrooks. The goodness and fascination of decay and death have to be faced. The Romantic enchantment has to have its consummation. The world must be destroyed by it and then, from the ashes, a rebirth of love and hope is possible. Hans Castorp, the commonplace German burgher, susceptible to the will to corruption through his love for music and his respect for illness and death, spends the seven years preceeding the First World War on this mountain. He is able to return to the ordinary world only when it, too, is shaken by the forces that have been at work among the inmates of the sanatorium. The cataclysm of the War provides the fulfilment of Mann's apocalyptic Romanticism.

The novel is modelled on the *Bildungsroman*, a novel of a hero's wanderings, education, trials and eventual return home with an extended understanding that belies the appearance of a simple cycle. Mann's hero, Hans Castorp, is a remarkably ordinary young man, yet his journey is of Nietzschean proportions. It leads him into the depths of the Romantic enchantment and then, possibly, to a heroic renunciation of that enchantment. The intellectual tensions felt on the mountain, however, represent not only the philosopher's individual struggle but the contemporary world-wide struggle. The people who have the most intellectual influence on Hans Castorp are Settembrini, a liberal, free-thinking Italian who is in love with the idea of liberty, Naphta, a Jesuit who views the Italian's optimism and humanism as sentimental and shallow, who himself sees the world as essentially a battlefield between matter and spirit, and Mynheer Peeperkorn, a Dutch coffee planter whose active enjoyment of life dwarfs the intellectuals' debates. Modelled, very freely, on Mann's brother Heinrich, the Marxist critic Lukács, and Gerhart Hauptmann respectively, these figures represent the various Western attitudes that were fighting for prominence in Germany. Mann found his brother's love for freedom ultimately despotic, and they quarrelled over their opposing views of Germany's part in the First World War; in Settembrini, the emptiness of Heinrich Mann's libertarian views is underlined by the Italian's flamboyant rhetoric of courage combined with his physical weakness. In *Meditations of a Non-Political Man*, written partly as a defence against Heinrich's attacks upon his acceptance of Germany's position in the First World War, Mann praises Lukács's early work *Die Seele und die Formen* in which he emphasises the importance of containing aesthetic ideals by life values; but Naphta distorts this theory so that life values are governed by aesthetic ideals. Only Hauptmann's physique, Mann repeatedly insisted, was used for Mynheer Peeperkorn, and the character certainly exhibits nothing of the playwright's concern for the social tragedy.

These European characters are themselves tied to the mountain; and the sanatorium itself, with its cyclical, unprogressive time, its idleness, exoticism and mysterious passions, represents the Eastern influences to which Germany was at that time susceptible, and which added to the confusion of her national definition. Yet though Hans Castorp's life in the sanatorium presents an allegory of Germany's spiritual life, the abnormality of his environment is essential to his tale. It is disease which allows the German youth to attain his special understanding. The air on the mountain is good for disease—that is, it encourages disease to exhibit its symptoms, so that Germany's *malaise* appears in a vivid, concentrated form. Moreover, disease provides freedom from the constraints of practical, respectable life. Life in the Berghof Sanatorium is not only a holiday from work, but a moral holiday as well; liberated from life, Hans Castorp can investigate, with impunity, Romanticism's passions and fascinations.

In *The Magic Mountain* Mann makes disease a central Romantic concept. In *Death in Venice* Aschenbach's vision of the reeking jungle that leads to his restless travels and, finally, to the abyss of his own imagination, mirrors the source of the disease which sweeps through Venice. Aschenbach's yearning for a widening of the inner barriers is a desire for the dissolution of his personality. Mann takes this desire for dissolution out of the usual Romantic schema in which dissolution is seen as spiritual release, and presents this desire as desire for spiritual and physical decay. Mann wants to expose the corruption inherent in a longing for release; in *The Magic Mountain* its spiritual aspect is undermined even more thoroughly than in the earlier novella. Here, the love of beauty, the mystical yearning, which can go wrong and result in decay, is superseded by the love of decay itself:

But in the first storey Hans Castorp stopped suddenly, rooted to the spot by a perfectly ghastly sound coming from a little distance off round a bend in the corridor. It was not a loud sound, but so distinctly horrible that Hans Castorp made a wry face and looked wide-eyed at his cousin. It was coughing, obviously—a man coughing; but coughing like no other Hans Castorp had ever heard and compared to which any other had been a magnificently and healthy manifestation of life: a coughing that had no conviction and gave no relief, that did not even come out in paroxysms, but was just a feeble, dreadful welling up of the juices of organic dissolution [. . .]Hans Castorp could not get over the coughing he had heard. He kept repeating that he could see right into the gentleman rider's vitals; when they reached the restaurant his travel-weary eyes had an excited glitter.

Chapter I, pp. 12–3

He might, indeed, be listening to *Tristan und Isolde* as Nietzsche described the opera's effect in *The Birth of Tragedy*; his ear is aware of the secret, deep inner functions of the world, and his consciousness is overwhelmed by the revelation.

To make a connection between a ghastly, transfixing sound of coughing and a transfixing beauty is in itself ironic, but Mann increases the tension of this identification by continually setting up an opposition between the sympathy disease demands and the frantic comedy of its practical difficulties. Joachim tells the new visitor that in winter, when the inmates of the various mountain sanatoriums die, the bodies have to be carried down on a bobsled. This news arouses in Hans Castorp an uncontrollable and embarassing fit of laughter: Romanticism's fascination with death, when applied to actual death, is confused by death's ugliness and absurdity. Hans Castorp, as an incipient Romanticist, believes there is something ennobling and edifying about death and disease. He is offended to see that severe disease occurs in coarse, common people. He believes that a corrupt body should make one more spiritual, but Settembrini, the humanist who pretends to value all life (though in fact he underestimates the power of the darker, destructive aspects of human nature) says that a diseased person is primarily body, for disease brings a person's physical aspects to the forefront of his consciousness and that therefore, on the contrary, disease is degrading. The behaviour of the sanatorium patients supports Settembrini's claim. This undermining of Hans Castorp's initial regard for disease, however, gives way to a more profound regard for disease. Its indignities and horrors actually increase its fascination; and this attraction to that which is inherently repulsive, reveals a basic and undeniable impulse to corrupt and destroy one's self.

One patient in the sanatorium, Herr Ferge, a Russian insurance investigator who would, in normal life, have had no extraordinary experiences whatsoever, has a lung operation without general anaesthetic, and he could feel the surgeon's hands on his inner organs. He had not imagined that such torments existed outside hell. It seems to him forbidden to have one's pleura touched; yet during the operation he heard himself laughing—not as a human being laughs, but in a devilish way, because the touch on his inner organs was like a disgusting tickle. The weird, cold vividness of this description is disturbing, and it does convey the impression of a sensation both horrible and hypnotic, of a sensation that is hellish not because it is painful but because it is repulsive; and its repulsiveness has moral overtones, even though the actual existence of a moral problem is uncertain. This uncanny sensation, however, to be more than a momentary effect, to fit into the network of Romantic fascination, must at least seem to be connected to some good. To be fascinated by the revolting simply because it is revolting would be merely an idosyncratic perversion. To make this a problem of general interest, the disgusting experience has to be shown to have some value, or its appeal to human needs must be explained.

Mann presents one argument for the love of the ugly and repulsive through Naphta. The Jesuit is contemptuous of health and beauty, and of Settembrini's notion of good as comfort, with all the crass materialism and industrialism such an identification implies. Naphta cites stories of saints' sufferings and the grotesque details of their tortures to prove that people crave the hideous and the repulsive. He believes that the driving force of the world is the hostility between spirit and matter. Beauty—the glorification of matter—is therefore antipathetic to the spirit, and people love ugliness—the denigration of matter—because it heightens their sense of the spiritual. He declares that people want to believe that salvation can be achieved only through pain, for only through physical degradation can they conceive spiritual beauty.

Naphta's views have some affinity to those of Nietzsche. The philosopher saw pain and adversity as necessary to achievement. He therefore rejected the notion of comfort as a good because comfort undermines creative achievement. The Jesuit, however, advocates pain not because it stimulates the imagination but because it satisfies the imagination. He is not interested in improving or invigorating the quality of mankind, for his view of the world as a constant battle allows for neither advance nor retreat. Naphta's similarity to the anti-religious Marxist emphasises the destructive conservatism in any world view based upon continuous hostility. Such a view, however apparently noble its purpose, is ultimately sadistic. Naphta's disdain for the material world is also a spiritual nihilism. His theory of truth (which he shares with the Marxist) is that truth is determined by man's interests and survival; and this theory, combined with his conservative and reductive suppositions about man's interests and salvation, paves the way—Settembrini rightly points out—to cruelty and suppression. Yet Settembrini himself is no less despotic. He cannot tolerate the Jesuit's emphasis upon the dark, corrupt aspect of man. He cannot permit, in his libertarian world, sympathy with the irrational forces of man's psyche. The two men are forced into a duel. Settembrini shoots into the air with a gallant flourish. His shallow optimism cannot be effective against the sadistic nihilist disguised as a man of spirit. Such a man, whose nature is deathly, is powerful against himself, too; and Naphta ends the duel by shooting himself.

The life-force which dwarfs these intellectual debates, however, also leads to death. Mynheer Peeperkorn claims to value life above everything—he values life itself, not as do Settembrini and Naphta, not only its brighter or its darker aspect. This indiscriminate love of life is largely sexual: Mynheer Peeperkorn describes life as a sprawling female to whom one is obliged to rise, and he sees impotence as the greatest affront to life's sensuous glory. He is not decadent or corrupt; he relishes the imediate and simple joys of life, and finds joy in commonplace things. Unlike Don Giovanni his enjoyment is not ruthless, but, as in the Don's case, dread and emptiness threaten him if his exuberance should fade. His inarticulate, enthusiastic exclamations are drowned by the roar of a waterfall; this overpowering of a greater natural force brings on impotence, and the following day Peeperkorn commits suicide. This ridiculous pagan figure is also bound by the attraction of death. As a life-force he wants all or nothing; and this refusal to compromise is ultimately destructive.

In this novel there is no fundamental resistance to the attractions of disease and death. If, somewhere along Hans Castorp's journey to the underworld, he came upon a dynamic 'no'—if, that is, the fascination with death, decay and disease was shown in the end to violate man's deepest interests and needs (as it is shown to do in *Doctor Faustus*) the spiritual drama would be more intense and the final apocalyptic vision might be more convincing. As it is, Mann's portrayal of the dæmonic sometimes has the cheapness of a haunted house atmosphere (as in the séance). In his treatment of disease, too, the thrill of horror, rather than horror itself, emerges. Disease, as Mann presents it, is something of a luxury; it comforts one and protects one from life's responsibilities and decisions. There is no indication that the life-alienating effects of disease are directly, deeply painful, or that such alienation involves an absolute loss. In *Buddenbrooks* Mann showed artistic sensibility to cut one off from life, and his sympathies were on the side of artistic sensibility. In *The Magic Mountain* his view is not fundamentally changed. It is interesting to compare this novel with Solzhenitsyn's *Cancer Ward* which also describes the way illness cuts a person off from life, but this loss of interest is an undeniable human loss, and the characters fight to maintain their involvement with other people and with their work. Part of Solzhenitsyn's greatness arises from his understanding of the need to work and to love and to participate in one's immediate world, however unsatisfactory that world happens to be, as human strengths. This view is alien to Mann's imagination. At the time of Hans Castorp's visit to the sanatorium he is preparing for a career as an engineer for a shipbuilding firm. This prospective employment is shown to be thoroughly mediocre, and in abandoning his career for the mountain's licence, he is not seen to be abandoning anything of real value. In fact, Hans Castorp avoids being a totally commonplace burgher through his awareness that the world, as he knows it, is not worth the practical man's exertion; and his love for Clawdia Chauchat, the love that binds him to the mountain, is like a 'frightfully alluring dream of a man whose unconscious questioning of the universe has received no answer save a hollow silence'.[2] The fascination with disease, and the debilitating passion bred by disease, provide compensation for an empty life rather than a threat to ultimate fulfilment.

The battle between life and death forces, therefore, is itself ambivalently conceived, and Mann's moral resolution to life is not quite integrated with what in the novel is felt to be man's greatest good. The ambivalence results in uneven writing, for Mann presents the resolution in morally satisfactory (that is, life-oriented) terms, but in terms in which he does not quite believe. A visionary resolution between these forces is presented in the section 'Snow'. Hans Castorp has summoned up sufficient initiative and energy to learn how to ski, for the alpine landscape intrigues him and he defies the sanatorium's prejudice against active, individual exploration. First Mann introduces the keen nostalgia of winter, but then lapses into a merely virtuoso description. His presentation of the snow-covered mountains as comic and fairy-like is over-extended; it is meant to balance the awe and sublimity of the high Alps in the distance, but this careful balancing of opposing views defeats them both. Gradually, however, the finer, majestic aspects of the scene blend with the confusing, compelling death wish:

> The snow fell silently. Everything blurred more and more. The glance, as it sank into the padded nothingness, inclined one to slumber. A shiver accompanied this view of distant places, yet there could be no sleep purer than this in the ice-cold, this dreamless reprieve from any unconscious feeling of organic life, as little aware of an effort to breath this contentless, weightless, imperceptible air as is the breathless sleep of the dead.
>
> Chapter 6, p. 472

Here the danger and the enchantment are at one with the reverence. The identity is not a combination of opposites which cancel one another, but a successfully disturbing presentation of the seduction of stasis. Yet this tender release from consciousness and from the pressures of organic life, is only one face of the death-wish; its other aspect is violent and destructive: the snowstorm continues to come as a 'mad dance, a white–dark, a monstrous dereliction' and Hans Castorp craves for contact with these violent, desolate mountains. But amid this wild, inhuman landscape, he feels his heart beating: 'A naïve reverence filled him for that organ of his, for the pulsating human heart, up here alone in the icy void, alone with its question and its riddle'.[3]

The cross-references to Hans Castorp's beating heart extend from his feverish passion for Clawdia Chauchat to that paltry, grotesque organ Hofrat Behrens describes whose function can be summed up as dissolution; but here the immediacy of Hans Castorp's organic humanity overcomes the distrust and ambiguity felt in the associated themes. The organic burden is straightforwardly embraced in protection against the seductive and destructive alpine landscape.

Subsequently, however, Mann forces a resolution upon Hans Castorp's musings. The young man rejects the uncanny, anti-organic perfection of the snow-flakes, and then sets out to lose his way in the white expanse of the mountains, which is so much like the expanse of the sea. Like the sea in *Death in Venice*, this cold desert represents the imagination which, for Mann, magnetises the elemental wildness and excesses of human nature, and is more appealing than normal human fulfilment. While Hans Castorp presses close to a hay-hut to keep warm, while he tries to resist the temptation to sleep—a sleep which would be his death—he has a hopelessly trite vision of young lads and lasses fishing, riding, engaging in archery, eating grapes and generally doing their best to present a Neoclassical image of the harmony between beauty and spirit, and what Mann calls a high seriousness without austerity. This happy vision is replaced by a disgusting scene within a temple where two old hags dismember a child and fight over the remains. In horror Hans Castorp wakes, but he continues to muse in a dream-like trance. He concludes that neither Settembrini, who insists upon the unqualified dignity of man, nor Naphta, who advocates man's degradation, is correct. From love and sweetness alone, he now realises, not from death and destruction, can beauty and civilisation arise; but one must nonetheless give recognition to the blood sacrifice, to the destructive will, and one must keep faith with one's connection with death, with one's longing for dissolution and release, but one must also prevent these darker tendencies from dominating one's thoughts.

This vision is similar, in its Neoclassical representation and its themes of harmony versus destructiveness, to Aschenbach's dream in which he believes he is waging a successful battle against desire until a terrifying howling, interspersed with sweet flutelike tones, infects him with savage lust. The allegory of Aschenbach's dream has an effectiveness lacking in Hans Castorp's vision, because the dream in *Death in Venice* clearly defines the battle that is actually waged within the writer's soul, whereas Hans Castorp's vision lacks the real spiritual tension that would make it a plausible drama. Hans Castorp is merely musing upon various theories about human nature; he himself stakes nothing upon the battle. Furthermore, Aschenbach's dream, while it reveals his emotional situation, also plays a part in the emotional drama; for, from this point, his unconscious and primitive will dominate him. But the vision in *The Magic Mountain* remains isolated from the other influences at work upon the youth. The 'healthy' compromise with death, which is proposed at the conclusion of Hans Castorp's vision, has no real bearing upon his life; it soon fades from his memory for, being without content, it cannot continue to guide his thoughts or his behaviour.

When, in *Death in Venice*, the writing is uneven, there is a point made by the discrepancy, which is not the case in *The Magic Mountain*. After having tried but failed to speak to Tadzio—that is, after failing to establish a normal and respectable relationship with the boy—Aschenbach's sleep is fitful, and he wakes early:

> in the faint greyness of the morning a tender pang would go through him as his heart was reminded of its adventure; he could no longer bear his pillow and, rising, would wrap himself against the early chill and sit by the window to await the sunrise. Awe of the miracle filled his soul newly risen from sleep.[4]

But as Aschenbach is unable to absorb this fresh responsiveness into his over-disciplined, detached consciousness, the language in which his thoughts are presented amalgamates his academic classicism with an uncontrolled sensuousness. The result is both sentimental and obscene:

> At the world's edge began a strewing of roses, a shining, a blooming ineffably pure; baby cloudlets hung illumined, like attendant amoretti, in the blue and blushing haze; purple efful-gence fell upon the sea, that seemed to heave it forward on its welling waves; from horizon to zenith went quivering thrusts like golden lances, the gleam became a glare; without a sound, with godlike violence, glow and glare and rolling flames screamed upwards, and with flying hoof-beats the steeds of the sun-god mounted the sky.[5]

He feels the glory of the sun kiss his eyelids and forgotten feelings of his youth, which have been suppressed by the cold discipline of his art, now return—but they are strangely changed, and he recognises them with a 'puzzled, wondering smile'. The transformation of innocence into savagery is beyond his understanding. His rational mind cannot tease out the various strands of his emotions, and the bewilderment defeats him, and the confusion is revealed in the language.

The various images are forced upon Aschenbach by the conflict between his thwarted impulses, his discipline and his newly awakened passion; but Hans Castorp's musings are often presented in highly schematic images, without convincing participation in or expression of the character's emotional drama. Connections between science and dæmonic investigations, or between death and music, are thrust forward by a memory or simile or repetition of a character's gesture.

The darkened room in which the séance is held reminds Hans Castorp of the darkened X-ray laboratory which, in turn, has been said to be similar to Faust's study. When Hans Castorp looks at his own skeleton and realises, for the first time, that he will actually die, his face assumes the sleepy and pious expression he habitually wears as he listens to music. This use of *leitmotif* forces rather than explores the associations. It does not justify or explain the connections between music, death, science and the dæmonic.

The lack of dramatic necessity in Hans Castorp's confrontations with death and decay is consistent with Mann's presentation of such preoccupations as indulgences. It is boredom and discontent that corrupts the inmates of the sanatorium—not the painful, inescapable soul conflict that destroys Aschenbach. In this novel Mann is interested in the languid effect of Romantic fascination, and the fascination of indulgence itself. Loving, rapt attention to detail indicates in itself the sinister nature of an object. Hans Castorp's persual of his thermometer—which is his membership card to the sanatorium and therefore to the world of licence and irres-ponsibility—provides a delight which signals danger:

> Smiling he took up the case and opened it. The glass instrument lay like a jewel within, fitted neatly into its red velvet groove. The degrees were marked by red strokes, the tenths by black ones; the figures were in red and the tapering end was full of glittering quicksilver.
>
> Chapter 4, p. 167

Also, the attention given to the gramophone indicates an importance far beyond that of a mere mechanical object; through the almost comically rich description of the object Mann makes the gramophone itself uncanny:

> This was a case finished in dull ebony, a little deeper than broad, attached by a cord to an electric switch in the wall, and standing chastely on its special table [. . .] You lifted the pretty bevelled lid, which was automatically supported by a brass rod attached on the inside, and there above a slightly depressed surface was a disc, covered with a green cloth, with a nickelled rim, and a nickelled peg upon which one fitted the hole in the centre of the hard-rubber record [. . .] The wonder-box seemed to seethe; it poured out the chimes of bells, harp, *glissandi*, the crashing of trumpets, the

long rolling of drums [. . .] He saw in his sleep the disc circling about the peg, with a swiftness that made it almost invisible and quite soundless. Its motion was not only circular, but also a peculiar sliding undulation, which communicated itself to the arm that bore the needle, and gave this too an elastic oscillation, almost like breathing, which must have contributed greatly to the *vibrato* and *portamento* of the stringed instruments and voices.

Chapter 7, pp. 636–7

The most compelling object on the mountain, however, the most vivid embodiment of lawlessness and intrigue and disease-ridden loveliness, is Clawdia Chauchat; and the features of her face are meticulously recorded, for the detail itself reflects Hans Castorp's fascination with the face:

It was an unusual face, and full of character [. . .] its mystery and strangeness spoke of the unknown north, and it teased the curiosity because its proportions and characteristics were somehow not easy to determine. Its keynote, probably, was the high bony structure of the cheek-bones; they seemed to compress the eyes—which were unusually far apart and unusually level with the face—and squeeze them into a slightly oblique position, while at the same time they seemed responsible for the soft concavity of the cheek, and this, in turn, resulted in the full curve of the pouting lips. Then there were the eyes themselves: the narrow 'Kirghiz' eyes, whose shape was yet to Hans Castorp a simple enchantment and whose colour was the grey-blue or blue-grey of distant mountains; they had the trick of sidewise, unseeing glance, which could sometimes melt them into the very blue of mystery and darkness.

Chapter 4, p. 146

The objects that fascinate seem also to hypnotise, and desire is almost no more than a desire to be enchanted in his rapt, passive manner. This rapture breeds idleness and stagnation which, in turn, provide a breeding ground for passion and enchantment. Fascination is like a door closing upon the normal world and normal activity; and, in isolation and idleness, fascination becomes frenzied excitement. It is when Hans Castorp is resting in bed, having been proclaimed to be ill, that his attraction to Clawdia becomes an overwhelming infatuation:

The day, artificially shortened, broken into small bits, had literally

crumbled in his hands and was reduced to nothing [. . .] In each
hour of his diminished day he thought of her: her mouth, her
cheek-bones, her eyes, whose colour, shape and position bit into his
very soul [. . .] Possessed of these thoughts, his hours passed on
soundless feet [. . .] Yes, he felt both terror and dread; he felt a
vague and boundless, utterly mad and extravagant anticipation, a
nameless anguish of joy [. . .]

                                        Chapter 5, pp. 192–206

The misgiving and the anguish are essential to this passionate
infatuation. Passion in spite of the world's opposition, passion which
battles with self control, passion which defies consequences are
common themes for the Romanticist; but Mann presents as the point
and danger of Romantic passion not its disregard for the world or for
ordinary life but its will to destroy ordinary life and discipline. Mann
is not interested in specific social contexts which thwart specific
passions. There is no social or indeed any external ban against Hans
Castorp's love for Clawdia, for there are no moral restraints on the
mountain. He keeps his distance from her until just before she leaves
the sanatorium not because circumstances frustrate his passion but
because his passion craves this secrecy and isolation. Only a passion
which reaches out into the world, towards another person, can suffer
from the more usual Romantic constraints of the world's censure. In
Mann it is passion that censures the world—the total normal world.
Passion cannot partake of spoken language, for language is tied to
reason and rational communication; passion communicates only with
smiles and glances, and would be destroyed by speech. Passion rejects
the world because it sees itself as the greatest good: 'But he was
enraptured not so much because she looked so charming, as because
her charm added strength to the sweet intoxication of his brain, the
intoxication that willed to be, that cared only to be justified and
nourished'.[6] Passion is a longing to intensify desire, not to satisfy it.
The drama of passion is a drama of the inward, isolating, destructive
will and of purely private joy.

As in *Death in Venice* the precarious balance between the physical
and the spiritual is a prominent theme, though in this novel the
relation between the two seems to be total opposition; whereas, in the
novella, there was at least a possibility that beauty—a material,
sensuous manifestation—would lead to or express the spirit. Here the
sensuous, even in its most promising state, borders on the disgusting.
Hans Castorp's first acquaintance with sensual love in the sanatorium

is made as he hears, from the next room, sounds of vulgar, playful lovemaking. And the entire subject of physical love is treated with this false objectivity, this half-unwilling voyeurism. Sexual love is deliberately taken out of the more usual contexts of affection and family bonds and breeding. In investigating sexual love among the diseased inmates of the sanatorium, Mann presents such love as ultimately perverse. As Hans Castorp admires the fine upward curve of Clawdia's arm he muses upon the efforts women take to achieve the illusion of beauty—efforts, he feels, which would be justified only if such illusion led to the preservation of the species, but which are immoral if the woman is diseased and therefore unfit for mother-hood. This attitude obviously extends to sex beyond the walls of the sanatorium, for it implies that attraction is illusion and that its only justification is propagation. The distaste with all physical love and the sense that it is never healthy, is underlined by the fact that while Hans Castorp is admiring Clawdia's arm and considering the immorality of beauty in a woman unfit for childbearing, he is listening to Dr Krokowski (the assistant director of the sanatorium, whose interests range freely over forbidden areas—hypnotism, psychoanalysis, som-nambulism, and the supernatural) lecture on the absurdity of physical love and its proneness to perversion. There is, the doctor says, a continual battle between chastity and love; and if chastity wins, then love emerges as symptoms of a disease. In a subsequent lecture, Krokowski suggests that love itself is a disease. His theory is that there is a poisoning, a sort of auto-infection of the organism caused by the disintegration of some as yet unknown substance which is present everywhere in the body. The products of this disintegration operate like an intoxicant upon the nerve centres of the spinal cord, with an effect similar to that of certain poisons, such as morphia or cocaine. Such is the chemistry of love, which explains its feverish, stagnant qualities.

Feverish and stagnant: Mann focuses upon the properties of love that Romanticism endorses both advertently (feverish—through Romanticism's esteem for intensity) and inadvertently (stagnant—through the Romanticist's desire to maintain intensity and therefore his need to avoid distractions and fluctuations of feeling). He presents qualities which combine the worse possible connotations of these terms, and continues to insist upon the attraction and power of such qualities. It is not that Mann actually endorses Krokowski's views. Clearly he shows the sadism that motivates the doctor's theories and the corruption in the will to place everything in a corrupt light.

Nonetheless, Krokowski's poison has a truth, in Mann's view, for it enforces the criticisms of love which emerge from the novel as a whole. As the assistant director lectures he continually repeats the word '*Liebe*' and the very sound of the word becomes grotesque:

> the slippery one-and-a-half syllables, with its lingual and labial, and the bleating vowel between—it came to sound positively offensive; it suggested watered milk, or anything else that was pale and insipid . . . He demolished illusions, he was ruthlessly enlightened, he relentlessly destroyed all honour in knowledge, he allowed no room for sensitive belief in the dignity of grey hairs or the innocence of tender children.
>
> Chapter 4, p. 127

Mann does not question the shaky assumptions upon which Krokowski's dismissal of innocence and honour are based. First, the obscene aspect is proposed as a point against the sentimental notions of the dignity of grey hairs and the innocence of the child. 'Dignity' and 'innocence' thereby imply either sexual ignorance or disinterest, and the assumption is that the existence of sexual feelings actually does undermine dignity and innocence. Secondly, the assumption that Krokowski's chemical analysis of love actually explains love in a way that makes an emotional or spiritual account of love either false or irrelevant, contains a philosophical confusion. Krokowski's account of love mingles chemical and normative terms. If his explanation of love's chemistry was accurate, the only thing it would show is that some substance breaks down and stimulates the nerves and that such stimulation is similar to the effect of certain other substances, specifically poisons or narcotics. To call this a case of auto-infection, however, or to call the process by which the substance is broken down 'dissolution', and to use the terms 'infection' and 'dissolution' in anything other than a description of a chemical process—in short, in a moral sense—is to equivocate. Furthermore, there is no reason to suppose that the chemical account of love supersedes or makes irrelevant the human or emotional aspect of love. At most, from Krokowski's arguments, one could say that certain chemical processes accompanied love; but love, initially, can only be identified as an emotion; the chemical process allegedly accompanying the emotion cannot be argued to provide a truer picture of love than does the emotion by which the chemical process is isolated. Emotions cannot be understood outside the context of subject and object; they cannot therefore be defined in chemical terms, even if it should be discovered that a certain chemical process always accompanied certain emotions.

Repeatedly Mann overestimates the relevance of chemical explanation to descriptions and evaluations of emotion. The Hofrat's scientific analyses of the skin tissue, as Hans Castorp admires the skin tones in the Hofrat's portrait of Clawdia, pretends to supplant the immediate sensuous appreciation of skin and to make that sensuousness appear something like a cheat because skin tones, the object of Hans Castorp's admiration, are susceptible to cold, detailed scientific explanation. Yet to give a chemical analysis of the paints on a canvas would not be to explain away or to undermine the aesthetic qualities of the painting, and a purely physical description of skin tissue does not deny the reality of its sensuous properties. Again, when Hans Castorp asks the director, 'What is body?' Mann actually seems to believe Behrens has answered the question in a way that has some bearing upon the spiritual and emotional capacities of the human being when he says that the human body is mostly water, a little protein, fat and salt; and when the Hofrat describes life as combustion, a breaking down of substances, and therefore as decay, the moral dissolution of Hans Castorp's passion for Clawdia is thereby marked as a counterpart of life's chemical process. Behrens's definition in fact denies the human or spiritual reality of anything that involves a physical response. As the Hofrat discusses the various reactions of the skin, Hans Castorp says that he does not get gooseflesh only when he has unpleasant sensations, but also when he listens to music. Behrens explains that the body is totally uninterested in the content of the stimulus: one might get gooseflesh from the repulsive sensation of being tickled by minnows as easily as from a confrontation with the Holy Ghost; the body's response is the same in each case. Mann often accompanies a description of Hans Castorp's emotional state with a reference to the Hofrat's various analyses of physical responses, and this reference is meant to deflate Hans Castorp's emotional state, to show that it is merely a physical response and that the emotional or spiritual value is illusory. Yet the fact—if it is one—that the body's responses to various stimuli are identical, simply shows the poverty of purely physical descriptions and their inability to indicate spiritual or emotional differences; it does not prove the emotional or spiritual content of such states to be illusory.

Mann does not actually deny the possibility of spirituality in emotion. He claims to find the image of spiritual emotion irrefutably compelling, yet he is suspicious of the value or reality of this vision. As Hans Castorp listens to the final duet of *Aïda* in which Radames and Aïda sing of their unity in heaven, it seems to him so beautiful that Aïda has come to die with her lover. The real, objective fact, however, is that two bodies, their lungs filled with pit gas, will die and putrefy and become two skeletons totally indifferent to one another. In spite of this, Mann says, the music provides an irrefutable alleviation of the physical horror. The undeniable comfort of the music, then, is seen to be opposed to the real, objective situation. The spiritual vision is endorsed, but only as a perverse stand against reason.

At one point Mann says that the physical and the spiritual can be resolved, that, in fact, it is impossible to make a clearcut division between the spiritual and the passionate, and that in the most frenzied infatuation there is *caritas*. As proof, he offers Hans Castorp's willingness to support Clawdia's attachment to Mynheer Peeperkorn. The support, however, is totally ineffective—perhaps even destructive. Moreover, this hopeful resolution is undercut by the overall picture of Hans Castorp's passion. It is an isolating, destructive passion, interested in its own enchantment, not in the other person's wellbeing.

Mann takes every opportunity to underline the repulsive aspects of that which fascinates and attracts. He defines passion as the organic sympathy, the sense embrace of that which is doomed to decay; and thus he mocks the Romantic image of passion as an eternal soul-embrace. The emphasis on decay—on decay in its most physical, disgusting aspects—does not, however, enable him to conquer his Romantic imagination. Decay does not diminish passion, but heightens it. In the world of *The Magic Mountain* excitement feeds upon decay; there is no possibility of healthy passion—either morally or physically healthy—because passion is aroused only in disease and only by something that is diseased or decaying. In *Death in Venice* disease was a symbolic manifestation of Aschenbach's inner life; in this novel it has become a real object of desire and fascination.

The Romanticist's desire for dissolution has been wrest from its metaphorical setting; the desire for dissolution is no longer seen as a longing for mystical union but for literal dissolution, with all the ghastliness of decay. Yet at the end of this novel in which, ceaselessly, the total deadliness of the Romanticist's desires has been exposed, Mann proposes the possibility of redemption through a cataclysm of death and destruction. His relentless criticism of Romanticism has resulted only in a corrupt Romanticism, and Mann ends by endorsing the Romantic schema of love arising through utter annihilation.

The final section of the novel presents a naïve and sentimental picture of a battlefield on which courageous young men, who crave neither the food nor the sleep they have been denied, pass willingly through mud and flame and explosions. Hans Castorp is among them. The First World War has shaken him from the idleness and indulgence of the mountain sanatorium, as it has shaken that world which answered his need for meaning with only a hollow silence. The cataclysm of destruction and death is proposed as a resolution of the death-disease fascination.

As Hans Castorp passes across the battlefield he has on his lips a song from Schubert's *Die Winterreise*, 'Lindenbaum,' and this song represents the paradox of Romanticism. The sentiments expressed by the song seem to be the sanest in the world. The song expresses the desire for rest and comfort and release from pain. For one moment, Mann says, the song provides refreshment which seems human and healthy, but the refreshment lasts only for a moment: 'it was the fruit of life, conceived of death, pregnant of dissolution'.[7] It begins with true sadness and longing and tenderness, but the expression of these sentiments is so striking, so beautiful, that the beauty leads to soul enchantment. Sorrow is no longer seen as a human ill, but as a fine excuse for beautiful expression. The beauty contains a longing which is a longing for release, for death. The song, in short, begins in life and conflict, and then leads to the Romantic impasse. The only path out of Romanticism lies in self-conquest, in a conscience that overcomes this seductive languor; but, Romanticist that he was, it was only in death that Mann could imagine resolution and rebirth: 'It was so worthy, one could die for it, this enchanted song. But he who died for it, really died no longer for it, and was a hero only because in dying he lay the groundwork for the new, the new word of love and the future in his heart'.[8]

Mann tried to defend himself against the allegation that he was hostile to life by citing (in a letter to Joseph Poten, 5 February 1925) his relentless mockery of death's dignity in *The Magic Mountain*. For all its indignity, however, death is no less fascinating and attractive; and, in conclusion, Mann gestures towards hope through this 'world-feast of death', and 'wicked feverish lust'. There is a clear parallel here with the end of *Götterdämmerung*, where Brünnhilde's love motive arises from the deluge of the Rhine; yet love and passion, in Wagner's *Ring*, have been shown to be positive, revitalising forces.

whereas, in *The Magic Mountain*, Mann has presented them as debilitating and destructive influences. His concluding, hopeful vision is as unsatisfactory, as untrue to the substance of this work, as would be the suggestion of redemption through love at the end of Strauss's *Salomé*.

5 Mann and Lawrence

A nearly random selection of quotations from *Women in Love* will show that Lawrence shares with Mann an interest in the dæmonic and ambivalent, a concern to measure the uneven value of that which attracts, a fascination for that which corrupts and destroys and for the peculiar flavour of forbidden attraction, and the view that passion destroys the self. As Gudrun watches Gerald at his sister's wedding, she sees that

> in his clear northern flesh and his fair hair was a glisten like sunshine refracted through crystals of ice . . . His gleaming beauty, maleness, like a young, good-humoured, smiling wolf, did not blind her to the significant, sinister stillness in his bearing, the lurking danger of his unsubdued temper.
>
> 'Sisters', p. 15[1]

and, having watched him for some time, she 'rose sharply and went away. She could not bear it. She wanted to be alone, to know this strange, sharp inoculation that changed the whole tenor of her blood'.[2]

The studio Gudrun and Gerald's young sister Winifred use for their art work has for Gerald 'the effect of a rather sinister richness' in which he can lose himself, and in the Austrian Tyrol Gerald determines that

> he would keep the unfinished bliss of his own yearning even through the torture [Gudrun] inflicted upon him. A strange, deathly yearning carried him along with her. She was the determining influence of his very being, though she treated him with contempt, repeated rebuffs and denials, still he would never be gone, since in being with her, even, he felt the quickening, the going forth in him, the release, the knowledge of his own limitation and the magic of the promise, as well as the mystery of his own destruction and annihilation.
>
> 'Snowed-Up', p. 502

Indeed, the imagery and language which express Mann's and Lawrence's sympathies with death ('the magic of promise', 'sinister stillness', 'sinister richness', 'strange, deathly yearning' are phrases that would be perfectly at home in *The Magic Mountain* or *Death in Venice*), the two novelists' respective assessments of the motivating power of the death-wish, their mingling of the repulsive and the fascinating are so strikingly similar and so unlike the interests of any other novelist that, despite their wide-ranging differences, a comparison of their approaches to the deathly and dæmonic throws light on the work of each.

It is, however, unlikely that either novelist himself would have recognised any common ground. Mann wrote to Carl Kerenyi (20 February 1943) that D. H. Lawrence was undoubtedly a significant phenomenon and characteristic of modern times, but that Lawrence's feverish sensuality had little appeal for him. Nor did Lawrence find Mann congenial. In an essay on Mann published in *Phoenix* (1936) Lawrence objected to Mann's formal precision. Form, Lawrence says, is not a personal thing like style, but an impersonal thing like logic. The human mind cannot fit absolutely the definite structure of a book and therefore Mann's form limits the human truths expressed in his works. Moreover, Mann's immense precision, his selfconscious artistry, Lawrence felt, stifled the rhythm of the work and prevented it from being a living investigation of mind, with blissful revelations of the unexpected and proud rises to discovery.

Lawrence did not only object to Mann's disciplined form and its effects, but also to his aesthete's view of life. Like Flaubert, Lawrence says, Mann feels vaguely that he has in him something finer than physical life can reveal. Physical life appears to Mann as a disordered corruption against which he can fight with only one weapon—his fine aesthetic sense, his feeling for beauty, for perfection, for a certain fitness that soothes him and pleases him, however corrupt the stuff of life might be. 'And so,' Lawrence concludes, 'with real suicidal intention, like Flaubert's, he sits, a last too-sick disciple, reducing himself grain by grain to the statement of his own disgust, patiently, self-destructively, so that his statement may at last be perfect in a world of corruption.'[3]

Lawrence's comments are based upon *Death in Venice*, but in all his works Mann does show a painstaking care not only in the writing but in the thematic structure which guides and limits his imagination. It is, however, a mistake to believe that Mann actually was disdainful of life in the way Flaubert was. Frequently Mann shows ordinary life as having little to offer, and his imagination explores its affinity with that which seems to resist practical interests and wellbeing; but this is not Lawrence's complaint. Lawrence believes that Mann is disdainful of the physical aspect of life; he believes that Mann sees sexual desire as corrupt, and that his aesthetic purpose is to create a perfect statement of this corruption. But though Mann's treatment of sexual desire does emphasise the pitfalls such desires present to man, he does not condemn sex. Rather, he shows it to be an area in which humanity is apt to become confused, and in which the ever-vague boundaries between good and evil, wellbeing and destruction, are prone to disappear altogether. *The Transposed Heads*, in which a woman's emotions and loyalties are confounded by the (literal) head swap between two men, one spiritual and the other sensual, both of whom she loves, is a grotesquely comic story that reveals the frequently utterly unresolvable tension between spiritual and sensual attraction. *The Black Swan*, in which a middle-aged woman mistakes signs of cancer for menstruation, and thus for rejuvenation, cruelly teases the notion that desires which seem good and natural have any counterpart in physical reality. *The Holy Sinner*, based upon one of the medieval *Gesta Romanorum* (which Leverkühn also uses in one of his compositions) is a masterly exploitation of the morbid combination of sensuality and piety, and it mocks the way a sensual bias can overtake any interest, however holy it may appear. Lawrence's faith in the wholesomeness and rightness of sexual desire may be more palatable to contemporary temperament, but it grossly pushes to one side the recalcitrant haunting of sex in man's consciousness.

The ambiguous flow of life, the tortuous combination of desire and value—of that which is felt to be good and that which is seen to be good—fully engages Mann's attention. Meticulously he balances a negative view against a positive one, revealing his uncertainty of each view with his irony. However, to set one view against another, as Settembrini and Naphta do, to outline the subtle negative and positive aspects of each view, is not to resolve the problem of the attraction of death and corruption, on the one hand, and the necessity of life on the other. Mann cannot resolve it because his attraction to the dæmonic was too strong, and it is in this attraction that his imagination shows a greatness Lawrence would deny him. Mann's intellect and his logic were on the side of life, but his imagination shows a living investigation of mind in its investigation of corruption and the death wish. It is an all-too-common thing, even among writers who want to advocate health, to have a deeper imaginative grasp of distortion and decadence than normality and goodness. Lawrence was not oppressed by his fascination of the sinister and destructive as was Mann, but his death-ridden, decadent lovers, Gudrun and Gerald, have a vividness and originality which the 'healthy' pair, Ursula and Birkin, share only when they, too, enter the dæmonic atmosphere in which good and evil are so confusingly mingled.

The amalgamation of pleasure and pain is frequent in *Women in Love*, as it is in *Death in Venice* and *The Magic Mountain*; and in Lawrence's work, too, such amalgamation is the result of passionate fascination, of intense, desirous love. Gerald says to Birkin:

> Gudrun seems like the end to me. I don't know—but she seems so soft, her skin like silk, her arms heavy and soft. And it withers my consciousness, somehow, it burns the pith of my mind . . . It blasts your soul's eye and leaves you sightless, yet you want to be blasted, you don't want it any different.
>
> 'Continental', pp. 494–5

What attracts one in such a case is corrosive to one's spirit, and the corrosion itself is desirable because it indicates close contact with the loved one and because this desire itself has self-destruction as its goal. The soft silken arms of Gudrun will destroy Gerald not only because they are powerful or because she wants to destroy him, but because his own desire for her annihilates his instinct for self-preservation. The desire to be blasted is the desire for a tremendous consummation. Such desire is destructive because, like the desire of Tristan and Isolde, its fulfilment can be imagined only when all boundaries between one's self and the other are dissolved. Mann shows Aschenbach's passion to destroy his personality and Hans Castorp's love to tie him to the isolating mountain; and Lawrence, too, emphasises the way insatiable longing takes possession of a person, and acts as a drug or imprisonment:

> Gerald winced in spirit seeing her so beautiful and unknown . . . There was something so revealed, she was beyond bearing to his eyes . . . And he felt he would not be able to avert her. And he writhed under the imprisonment.
>
> 'Threshold', pp. 315–6

Save for the extreme beauty and mystic attrativeness of this

distinct, strange face, she would have sent him away. But his face
was too wonderful and undiscovered to her. It fascinated her with
the fascination of pure beauty, cast a spell upon her, like nostalgia,
an ache . . . She wished his warm, expressionless beauty did not so
fatally put a spell on her, compel and subjugate her.

'Death and Love', p. 387

Naturally, Mann and Lawrence are not alone in treating passion as
a narcotic or subjection, but their emphasis upon the soul's dramatic
part in the subjugation and the inner will to dissolution is characteristic of a Romantic interest in passion. Furthermore, the susceptibility
to such fascination is given a similar analysis by each novelist. For just
as Hans Castorp's enchantment arises from his inability to find
meaning in the 'normal' world, so Gudrun's and Gerald's love is
embedded within their mutual attempts to stave off a terrifying
meaninglessness. Lawrence adds a further dimension to this destructive infatuation by showing it as a drama between two people, so
that destructive and self-destructive impulses are stimulated by
personal interaction, whereas Mann presents the drama as an isolated,
inner battle. He frequently indicates that such a passion would not
survive close personal contact. Aschenbach refrains from speaking to
Tadzio because the prosaic communication of speech would threaten
imagination's appreciation of the boy's beauty. To judge the boy—as
he would do if their communication was based upon the rational
plane—would be to lose his regard for him. This notion of passion or
infatuation as something that is so easily threatened by the normal
world reveals Mann's view of passion as, ultimately, a pathetic
fantasy. Passion, in Mann, is the occasion of decadence and self-
destruction; as an emotion, as an attempt to achieve human
connection, it is not interesting to him.

Mann's quasi-Platonic analysis of Aschenbach's decline (beauty
should lead to the divine, but beauty is perceived by the senses, and
the senses can be led astray by beauty until a sensuous appreciation of
beauty becomes sufficient unto itself and issues in sensuous debauch
rather than spiritual fulfilment) is unsatisfactory as a psychological
account of the writer's indisputable will to decline, and his explanation of Hans Castorp's death enchantment as a result of the world's
emptiness is incomplete. Lawrence, however, does investigate the
immediate and dynamic motivation toward self-destruction. His
psychology certainly would have impressed Freud; indeed, it is more
satisfying than Freud's work on the same subject. Freud wondered

and wondered how it was that there should be sadism in love—how love, which desires to preserve its object, could also desire to destroy its object. He concluded, in *Beyond the Pleasure Principle*, that there are two types of instincts—libidinal and death instincts—and that sadism is a death instinct which, through narcissism (or libidinal instinct directed towards one's self) is deflected from the person himself and made to seek an outer object. Lawrence vividly presents such a process (Freud does not) and, furthermore, Lawrence explains, as Freud does not, why it is the love object, and not some other outer object, that becomes the recipient of these impulses.

Aschenbach's self-destruction results partly from the energy he absorbs from the sea and sun and idleness but which he does not use in his art. In the writer's case, energy is directed to the imagination, and if the imagination is not disciplined as artistic creation it becomes debauchery. Lawrence's analysis of Gerald's self-destruction is similar, but less specialised; it does not pertain only to an artistic temperament. Gerald's impulses become self-destructive only when the outer world thwarts his aggressions. If he cannot direct his will towards the subjugation of the miners or a mare or a lover, these impulses lash back upon himself. His sadism, unsatisfied, fills him with a sense of death and torments him with his own emptiness—an emptiness that is not mere absence but which has a violent effect. While his father is alive Gerald's regard for the social structure, for respectable appearances and practical efficiency is nearly sufficient to keep his life in order; but his father's death shifts the responsibility of finding meaning onto himself, and his unquestioning faith in his social function is broken. The obsession with which he clings to Gudrun arises from his need to keep his mechanical drive, his need to exert power, from turning in upon himself. His approach to her is not straightforwardly sadistic. There is a true sense in which he needs her because he loves her and because only with her can he find comfort; but his love reaches a sadistic impasse because, in giving himself to her in love, he passes on to her his destructive impulses:

Into her he poured all his pent-up darkness and corrosive death, and he was whole again . . . And she, subject, received him as a vessel filled with this bitter potion of death . . . The terrible frictional violence of death filled her, and she received it in an ecstasy of subjection, in throes of acute, violent sensation.

'Death and Love', p. 388

The drama of destructive impulses is reciprocal, as it never is in Mann's works. Gerald chooses Gudrun partly because she does understand what he is doing. This understanding is one aspect of her fascination for him. Gerald's love, obviously, wearies her; she is weakened and filled with a sense of death because of the way he has used her, but 'the passionate, almost hateful fascination' revives in her, and she realises that her passion for him is not yet satisfied and perhaps can never be satisfied. This Romantic compulsion of unfulfillable longing forces her to accept a union with him, which is an acceptance of a deadly challenge.

Gudrun does not long for death directly, as Mann's characters often do; she is attracted by death because she is attracted to Gerald; she is actually attracted by his 'go', that is, his ability to direct his death-impulses outward, to make them aggressive, and she is willing to accept his death-impulses as proof of his strength. Only when she discovers that she can be stronger than he, does she resent him. In Mann's works the connection between love and death is made not because love is aggressive, but because it is passive. The longing is too great to bear; only in death will the yearning be both satisfied and sustained. For Mann the goal of such fascination is death, and the ultimate purpose of passion is to destroy the self—a destruction which in Wagner's *Tristan* seems noble but whose worth Mann continually questions. In *Women in Love* passion which seeks the dissolution of the self indicates desire for complete union with the other—and here the union is not mystic transfiguration but possession or domination. Therefore, self-dissolution can easily become violent, as it does in Hermione's case (she attacks Birkin because she cannot know him thoroughly, that is, she cannot mentally take possession of him) and in the case of Gerald, who tries to strangle Gudrun because she refuses to be his other half, his deathly half. But though Lawrence sees the death wish as an effect of various needs, fears and impulses rather than as a *donnée* of human desire, he shares with Mann an appreciation of the Romantic image of death, as an immensity of rich expectation. Ursula reflects:

death is a great consummation, a consummating experience. It is a development from life . . . to die is to move on with the invisible. To die is also a joy, a joy of submitting to that which is greater than the known . . . Life indeed may be ignominious, shameful to the soul. But death is never a shame. Death, like the illimitable space, is beyond our sullying.

'Sunday Evening', pp. 214–6

This indeed could read as a postscript to *Death in Venice*; for in the novella Mann shows a degeneration of the soul that cannot, in life, submit with dignity to that which is greater than itself. Death is the mitigation of his sordid defeat; it is the promise to which his love points. Ursula, however, finds death attractive not because her lover stimulates a death wish, but because he forces her towards life and growth, towards a dynamic contact that will disturb her equilibrium, which will destroy her individuality. Death appears to her as a means of preserving herself from violation; in death she will be untouchable and unchangeable. As Aschenbach dies, watching Tadzio point out to the vague immensity of the sea, he is fulfilling love's command; whereas Lawrence, in Ursula's case, presents the death wish as an escape from love's demands.

Gerald, too, in the end, seeks death not aggressively, but as rest and release. Gudrun resists him; she denies him an outlet for his destructive impulses, and the power–death urge breaks upon him. She has bolstered her strength through her attachment to the German artist Loerke—a distinctly un-Mannish artist in that he does not thrive upon illusion but he exults in the spirit of the practical world. Birkin and Gerald call him a sewer rat, for he is at home in corruption—not in a Mannish corruption of disease and passion, but in the corruption of industrialism. Mann's artists thrive upon ideals, but Loerke exposes ideals and celebrates the soullessness of industrialism. Loerke has no need of the spirit, and his acceptance of nihilism excites Gudrun, and this excitement gives her a sophisticated weapon against Gerald, who needs to camouflage his desperate hollowness. Gudrun sees Gerald as a *Dummkopf* because he cannot make his nihilism creative or aggressive; his nihilism becomes passive; it becomes a longing for stasis and peace.

It is within the strangely radiant, changeless and silent setting of the Tyrolean mountains that Gerald and Gudrun and Loerke confront the forces of death and destruction. The timeless frozen eternity of the setting acts as the Swiss mountain air in *The Magic Mountain*—that is, as a wonderful intoxicant of malevolent coldness, as a mingling of the weird, the quaint and the inhuman, crystalline grandeur, as a place whose elemental majesty stimulates the death wish and whose isolation grants special freedom. Like the patients of the Berghof

Sanatorium, Gudrun and Loerke remove themselves from real life. 'Their natures seemed to sparkle in full interplay', they enjoy a continuous game together, treating the world's major characters as their own marionettes, and when Loerke laughs at Gudrun's extravagance he himself is so absurd that she actually feels liberated by his teasing. In the isolated mountains Gudrun embraces a world of pure possibility, unhampered by commitment or decision or responsibility, a world as aimless and licentious as that of Mann's sanatorium, with a craving for freedom, for limitlessness, which is stimulated by the idea of death:

> Anything might come to pass on the morrow. And today the white, snowy iridescent threshold of all possibility. All possibility—that was the charm to her, the lovely, iridescent, indefinite charm—pure illusion. All possibility—because death was inevitable, and *nothing* was possible but death.
>
> 'Snowed-Up', p. 526

Gerald cannot compete in this world that thrives upon its own emptiness. He cannot survive the decay of spirit, as do Loerke and Gudrun. Something breaks in Gerald's soul; he sinks into the snow and sleeps the frozen sleep of death. There was a *Marienhutte* in which he might have saved himself—just as Hans Castorp saves himself by pressing close to a hay-hut—but the world no longer offers any object upon which he can vent his aggressions; these must be quieted, and they can be quieted only in death. Castorp survives the freezing storm in the Alps because he realises the need to keep his sympathy with death subordinate to life; whereas Gerald, before he collapses in the snow, finds a crucifix—the symbol of the worship of death and of the painful processes which lead to death.

The battle between Gerald and Gudrun takes place on the brink of nihilism. Such battles arise when the value of everything outside the self has been denied. There is nothing to live for in the world, nothing to satisfy the need for meaning and reverence and wonder. Only self-assertion and social standing remain real to Gerald. His will is as deadly mechanical as his efficiently run colliery. His continuous activity is a means of disguising lack of direction of his energies, and he craves the stimulus that will keep this activity, and this disguise, in order. In 'Rabbit' he is inflamed by Gudrun's sullen passion of cruelty; she seems like a 'soft receptacle of his magical, hideous white fire'. But it is not the idea of cruelty itself that excites him; rather, it is the stimulus and challenge and the direction it offers to his own aggression. It would be easy for Gerald to inflict pain upon Minette, the 'flower of mud' from Chelsea who longs to be subjected by him. If Gerald's impulses were sadistic, he would have chosen this delicate creature, but when he understands her willingness to be the object of his cruelty he realises he must leave her. Gerald's sadism can be satisfied only by a struggling, resisting victim because his sadism is not the desire for cruelty itself but a desire for challenging self-assertion— a challenge that will make him feel he is doing something with a purpose.

In *The Magic Mountain* Mann says of Hans Castorp that he is above the ordinary because he tacitly understands that his society provides no real meaning and, therefore, no reason for exertion, no direction for his energies. His love of Clawdia Chauchat has the indulgence and lovesick vagrancy of a man completely cut off from society, of a man who has no deep-rooted connection with the world around him. Aschenbach's decay, too, begins when he comes to question the significance of his socially honoured position and the truth of his art. His doubt undermines his discipline; it creates a longing for new stimulants and new directions, and such longing breeds infatuation and decay. In *The Magic Mountain* and *Death in Venice* inertia and dissolution enter at the point where, in *Women in Love*, sadism and self-destruction enter: both writers present spiritual corruption as an outgrowth of society's emptiness.

As with Mann, the licence that intrigues Lawrence and which corrupts some of his characters is not a specifically sexual licence, but a moral one. This corruption is a nihilism which denies the value of everything other than the satisfaction of one's own impulses, when one's impulses hold nothing sacred, and are aimless and excessive. Gudrun and Gerald exult in the forbidden freedom their relationship promises as they struggle with the rabbit—whose name is Bismarck, a name which both mocks the pretensions of the Prussian Bismarck and reveals their game as a serious power struggle. They are trying to catch the rabbit so that Gerald's sister Winifred can draw him ('Draw and quarter him?' Gerald jokes) and the animal scratches them both. Gudrun's wound seems to sear Gerald's brain; he feels that they share a dangerous, mysterious breadth of knowledge, for they understand one another's delight in this blood-game. The excitement they inspire in one another has no specific object, as would sexual desire. Their excitement is sheer recklessness and freedom. Their desire can never be satisfied because no object or pleasure could hold their esteem for any length of time: Gudrun would reduce its significance with mockery, and Gerald would prove his power over it and be done with it. They crave excitement and challenge, but they have destroyed the world's power to provide interest and stimulus. The best they can have, as a substitute for meaning, is a series of breathtaking moments. Soon Gudrun wearies of Gerald because his mechanical will and social position no longer distract her from the abyss of ennui. His power is merely a means of subduing the outer world, and the outer world is not worthy of exertion. Through Loerke, she learns to dismiss the world with a sneer. Initially, knowing everything inward was a bad show, she had believed in the value of appearances, but Loerke confirms her growing sense that appearances, too, are worthless, and that one can derive strength from the abolition of ideals. Neither Mann nor Lawrence can indeed offer a clearly positive resolution of this impasse. Birkin and Ursula come to some private settlement, but only by cautiously rejecting society (as soon as they become engaged they resign their respective positions), and Birkin says he would be happy to see a thorough destruction of humanity so that the real tree of life would be relieved of 'the most ghastly, heavy crop of Dead Sea Fruit'. In the works of these two novelists the path away from the fascination of death is both deadly (in Mann it is a world-feast of death) and vague.

The characters in *Women in Love*, as in *The Magic Mountain* and *Death in Venice*, are subject to forces of which they are not fully aware and which they often fear, for these are inward forces, arising from a character's own attraction to evil and destruction. One's impulses can lead one away from life, and the incipient awareness of the split between desire and well-being, is frightening: ' "Isn't it an amazing thing," cried Gudrun, "how strong the temptation is not to [marry]!" They both laughed, looking at each other. In their hearts they were frightened'.[4] Throughout the work there is an overwhelming sense (similar to the pangs of conscience and fear that disturbed Hans Castorp's infatuation and Aschenbach's gloating discovery of the extent of Venice's disease) that what one seeks as fulfilment will actually lead one to corruption and death. This is precisely what happens to Gerald, Gudrun and Aschenbach, and what nearly happens to Hans Castorp and Ursula.

The danger involved in pursuing one's desires is connected to the amalgamation of attraction and repulsion. In *The Magic Mountain* Mann shows the diseased and the grotesque as having an uncanny

fascination, and the sense of wanting to approach that which one is
inclined to reject, makes it impossible to trust the goodness of one's
desires. Lawrence's appreciation of the attractiveness of the sinister is
not less vivid than that of the German Romanticist:

> The heavy gold glamour of approaching sunset lay over all the
> colliery district, and the ugliness over-laid with beauty was like a
> narcotic to the sense . . . On the roads silted with black dust, the
> rich light fell more warmly, more heavily, over all the amorphous
> squalor a kind of beauty was cast, from the glowing close of the
> day.
> 'It has a foul kind of beauty, this place,' said Gudrun, evidently
> suffering from fascination. 'Can't you feel in some way, a thick,
> hot attraction in it? I can. And it quite stupefies me.'
>
> 'Coal-Dust', p. 128

And though Gudrun's compulsive fascinations are often set against
the more vital normality of her sister, Ursula, and Birkin—the
'healthy' couple—they are not free from this disturbing ambivalence:

> Ursula looked all the while at Hermione, as she spoke in her slow,
> dispassionate and yet strangely tense voice. A curious thrill went
> over the younger woman. Some strange, dark, convulsive power
> was in Hermione, fascinating and repelling.
>
> 'Carpeting', pp. 155–6

> He was almost afraid of the mocking recklessness of her splendid
> face. Here was one who would go to the whole lengths of heaven
> and hell, whichever she had to go. And he mistrusted her, was
> afraid of a woman capable of such abandon, such dangerous
> thoroughness of destructivity. Yet he chuckled within himself also.
>
> 'Mino', p. 171

Enough passages from *The Magic Mountain* and *Death in Venice* have
been quoted to show examples of similar mingling of destructivity
and attraction, foul and beautiful, glamour and magic, and stupe-
faction and narcosis. Lawrence, however, never gets lost in his delight
with iridescent decay; the sinister atmosphere is never indulgent or
gratuitous, as it sometimes is in *The Magic Mountain* and *Doctor
Faustus*, when things such as séances and naturalistic studies are allied
to the dæmonic.

At their best, both novelists show evil as emerging from life—not as anti-life, but as a lush growth, a reeking richness, containing a feverish abundance and vitality. Hence, destructive and death impulses combine so easily with a sense of goodness and fulfilment. Indeed, at one point, when musing over the question 'What is life?' Hans Castorp toys with the (quasi-Schopenhauerian) notion that life is an aberration, a pathologically luxuriant growth, consisting of desire and moving towards death. Hans Castorp's conclusion that one can only live by keeping faith with one's impulses towards death and destruction is mirrored in Lawrence's image of the river of corruption, running beside the river of health, which must be seen as part of life's current. An acceptance of life's undergrowth is healthier and richer than ignorance of it. Birkin explores the rank water plants from which Ursula, less certain of her capacity to respond well, shrinks. But there is danger, too, in this rank growth, which fascinates Gudrun, with a stagnant fascination. Birkin's knowledge is indeed shown to be precious; for when Hermione sees him copying the Chinese drawing in which the quick, vital goose emerges from the mud river, she feels her own limited understanding, and in jealous madness tries to destroy Birkin. Mann never achieved even this momentary, vivid sense of balance. Hans Castorp's vision lacks the richness of Lawrence's imagery, and though in *Death in Venice* his portrayal of the reeking, feverish undergrowth is unrivalled, he can show no quickening life arising from the swamp.

Though these two novelists made totally different uses of disease (for Lawrence it was merely a negative condition and was in no way connected to the ambiguously valuable dissolution and corruption) they share some attitudes towards it. Lawrence hated the modern trend of analytic psychology. He saw it (in *St Mawr*) as a means of tearing everything to pieces, as a search for what is nasty, as a dissection of mental secrets with a technique that is bound to make everything smell bad—just as Mann shows Dr Krokowski doing when his repetitions of '*Liebe*' make the word sound like an obscenity. Disease and suffering, according to both novelists, provide a good disguise for the sadist. Not only medical investigation, but sympathy for suffering, too, allowed satisfaction to the sadist. The exceedingly charitable Mr Crich seems to his wife like 'some subtle funereal bird, feeding on the miseries of the people. It seemed to her he was never satisfied unless there were some sordid tale being poured out to him, which he drank in with a sort of mournful, sympathetic satisfaction'.[5] And Mann sees sadism in Hans Castorp's merciful attention to the hopelessly ill people in the sanatorium: 'there was a malicious satisfaction he had in the blamelessly Christian stamp his activities bore—it was so clear that on no ground whatever, either military or humanistic or pedagogic, were they open to any serious approach'.[6] Sympathy becomes a disguise for delighted interest in pain. The motive is malicious not in the sense of wanting to inflict pain, but in the sense of wanting to torture oneself. In Mr Crich's case, self-torture is based upon guilt for the poverty of his workers and upon his morbid notion of Christian humility and charity. Hans Castorp's self-torture, however, is a substitute for love, because the disgusting allure of disease is similar to the deathly, ultimately corrupt force of passion. But though the English novelist could describe the horrid details of illness as well and as vividly as Mann, his attitude was one of complete, even excessive disgust—a disgust which marks rejection rather than fascination. Ursula despises Birkin's weakness while he is convalescing, and she asks him whether he does not find it totally humiliating to be ill. Mr Crich clings to life despite his hopeless illness, and this clinging is presented as mean and ignoble. He should let himself die, because death is a pure thing, beyond physical and spiritual disintegration. Thus Lawrence endorses the Romantic separation between disease and death, and shows death to be clean and sublime, whereas disease is physical and abhorrent. Mann, however, combines the notions of death and disease, using disease to emphasise his criticisms of Romanticism's penchant for death; but, in the end, he turns disease itself into a Romantic notion, and presents a Romanticism which compels as much by its horror as its goodness.

6 Myth and Resolution

Those aspects of Germany's Romanticism which Mann most feared—the glorification of instinct, a barbaric respect for heroism and disdain of death, belief in a folk-blood morality that cancelled the possibility of a humanist morality—were realised in the National Socialists' use of myth. This was a narrow racial mythology, in which rationality and liberal freedom were seen as shallow constraints upon the collective psyche and were therefore sacrificed to a feast of destructive forces. National Socialism found the elements of its mythology in Germanic myth, and in the most compelling Romantic realisation of those myths, Richard Wagner's *Der Ring des Nibelungen*. Though this work cannot be reasonably seen as a justification of a Nazi-style immorality, with its emphasis upon the self-destructiveness of greed, misrule and the bid for power, with its critical portrayals of Hagen's chilling, dæmonic hatred and Gunter's dishonourable subservience and Mime's pathetic weakness and Loge's destructive disdain (to give only a few examples), and though Wagner's exploration and employment of the death wish and his use of the theme of *ragnarök* (the final battle between gods and dæmonic forces in which all will perish) are not actually negative (cf. my chapter 3, 'The Death Enchantment'), this work helped to inspire and enforce the shallow, deadly political myth.

Mann saw that the Nazis' use of Wagner involved a misuse of the composer's works, but he also felt that the music's presocial, archaic—Romantic aspects lent themselves to misuse. Mann wanted to re-establish the myth along humanist lines; from primitive, popular, elemental ideas he would construct a biblical—mythical tale which would point to moral progress rather than to moral decline. He valued myth because it provided man with a kind of foreknowledge—not necessarily of specific events, but of the kinds of forces with which he will have to struggle, and of the various forms of victory and defeat. Also, myth informs man of various roles—as avenger, forgiver, provider, traveller—and gives individual character and behaviour a new dimension, for in mythical consciousness the individual's history becomes a re-enactment of a collective history. Archaic man, he suggests in his essay on Freud, lived with myth in the following way: he stepped back before doing anything, like a toreador poising himself for the death stroke; he sought examples in the past, and slipped into the past image or story as into a diving bell. In this way he plunged into the problems of the present, and in this way he both understood his life and found meaning in it.

In an address delivered to the Library of Congress (1942) Mann explained his impulse to write the Joseph novels as the desire to transcend the story of the individual. In a story that seemed to side-step the issues of the times, he wanted to use, as Wagner had, a combination of psychology, myth and symbol that was both timeless and modern. He planned to retell the Joseph story (influenced by Goethe's remark to Eckermann that he found the Bible's account too short) as a story about the creation of a certain type of human. He wanted to use myth not to celebrate its sympathy with the irrational elements of life but to show a resolution between the divisions within man, and to pave the way to a new humanism based upon this possibility of resolution and upon extension of sympathy through myth, that is, through the awareness of the individual's history as collective and representative.

The prologue to the four volumes, 'Descent into Hell', presents Mann's mythical stage through the neo-Platonic romance of the soul. Thus he introduces a transhuman model of conflict and resolution, and presents exemplary scenarios which will be repeated or re-enacted by his characters who will thereby break out of profane time and exist in what Mircea Eliade calls the Great Time or primordial time; for the individual action becomes that action upon which it is modelled, and the profane time and place are less important aspects of the action than its representational aspect. Therefore Mann suggests a different conception of personal identity, one in which personal identity is open-ended, so that each man sees himself as living through the history of another, and each event as bearing the significance of similar events. Mann denies the horror Nietzsche saw in the image of eternal recurrence, but feels that the individual's significance is confirmed by this representational identity. Moreover, he does not view the repetition as static, as Nietzsche did, but believes it permits room for human improvement. In the first volume he uses the notion of cyclical history in his method of narration. The story moves backwards—not in a straight backward line, but in flashback and progression, then flashback to a more distant point. *Tales of Jacob* opens eight years after Rachel's death, but then moves back, to the explanation of Jacob's attachment to Rachel's first son and the tension between Joseph and the sons of Leah. This tension involves the question of passing on the blessing, and Mann therefore returns to the story of Jacob and Esau. The story proceeds to Jacob's dwelling by the city of Schechem, and then returns to tell of the theft of the blessing from Isaac, and Jacob's flight to the land of Laban, so that the volume actually ends at the time of Rachel's death. This backward, cyclical movement of the narration makes the novel more rich, more dense, and provides a literary form for the mythical open-endedness of interpretation and meaning.

Mann's purpose in this tetralogy is uncharacteristically optimistic. Even imagination which, in all his other works, alienates one from life and disturbs any harmony there might be between desire (what one feels to be good) and morality (what one believes to be good), is in the Joseph novels a force working on life's behalf. Here imagination involves the ability to understand other people, not with Tonio Kröger's detached superiority, but with a sympathy that brings one closer to them and enables one to act with greater kindness and effectiveness. Here imagination is a moral force (as it eventually becomes, but only after a tremendous struggle, in *Doctor Faustus*) in the way it is able to see individual circumstance as representative, and through this representation the mythically conscious man can gauge its value and can draw upon the spiritual resources of the myth.

This use of myth as a moral and life-promoting mode of thought demands an irreducible belief in the story and the network of associations from which such understanding and assessment are derived. Mircea Eliade, in *Myths, Dreams and Reveries*, points out that among those groups of people where the myth provides a foundation of social life and culture 'the myth is thought to express the *absolute truth*, because it narrates a *sacred history*.'[1] The mythical story becomes exemplary and repeatable, that is, it serves as a model and justification for human actions, and lifts those actions out of profane time, because the mythical story is real and sacred: that is the point of its repetition, for the repetition is imitative. Of course there is a way of mythical thinking which does not involve such literal belief. There are artistic uses of the myth which use mythical material not because the original story is seen to be historic truth, but because the mythical themes have a power and conviction and depth of association which make the dramas true and representative not in virtue of actual history but in light of eternal laws of man and nature. But even in artistic uses, these eternal laws must have a sacred aspect, not necessarily in the sense of being laid down by a god, but in having a transhuman aspect, an awesome aspect, an aspect which transcends (though it may encompass) the psychological. This transhuman sense, this irreducible belief, is necessary to give a mythical story, or a folk tale, the power of myth in art.

Mann cannot always sustain this kind of belief. First, the form of the novel (as opposed to drama or opera), with its mass of secular and particular detail, is not suited to the essentially allusive quality of myth. Secondly, Mann frequently employs an ironic attitude towards his story; and though in myth characters can be ironic or situations can be ironic, the story itself must be presented in a totally serious light, for there is something necessary and irreducible in the story, and therefore irony towards the story itself is inappropriate. In his other works Mann uses myth alongside the individual, psychological story. Aschenbach's battle has obvious affinities and many references to Dionysian rites; and in *The Magic Mountain* certain behaviour becomes ritual—such as the taking of one's temperature and the everlasting meals—and the mythic pattern in such secular affairs is successful comedy. In the Joseph novels, however, the mythical themes are not auxiliary but substantial, and the success of the novels rests largely upon the success of mythical presentation. The highly detailed, circumstantial treatment endangers this success. Mann's attention to detail is often, in itself, a subject of his irony, as though he is uncomfortable with the story, as though mythical power can be sustained only at a distance. He tries to calculate, for example, the precise number of years which must have passed before Jacob left Laban's land if, as the Bible says, Joseph actually bowed down before Esau on the journey, because the story of his bowing down is inconsistent with the Bible's assertion that Jacob left Laban's land immediately after Joseph's birth. Mann also takes time to consider the precise place of Dinah in the list of Jacob's children, and in so doing he underlines the inaccurate—or, rather, the inactual—story by pretending to take the story very seriously.[2]

To pretend to treat the story as substantial history, however, is to pay lip-service to one aspect of mythical reality while undermining the mythical truth of which art makes use. If the eternal aspect of myth is to be realised, the story cannot be too definite. Detail presents a situation conditioned by arbitrary and merely contemporary forces. Furthermore, myth—as a richly symbolic tale—actually gains effectiveness by indeterminate or many-faceted explanation. The indefinite path by which Brünnhilde comes by her knowledge of Siegfried's part in the drama of the Ring and its curse at the end of *Götterdämmerung* actually reinforces the sense of an ultimately coherent, though darkly clouded world in which the characters move. The various explanations of the loss of Wotan's eye add to the significance of that loss; the uncertainty of a single account is the price paid for multiple interpretations. Events and motives in myth are over-determined as are dream images and dream patterns. Furthermore, the fact that Hagen must be approximately the same age as Siegfried, though Hagen seems much older, points to myth's use of age and event as a function of character rather than actual, prosaic history; for any production which made the two characters out to be the same age would be untrue to one or other of the characters. This type of inconsistency—profane inconsistency—is irrelevant to myth, where the reality resides in character type and the drama is one of forces rather than circumstance. Mann's own wry concern with detail is mirrored in Joseph's sophisticated questioning of the seriousness of re-enactments. If the circumstantial detail is important, and if belief in the mythical story depends upon its historic plausibility rather than upon its poetic power, then the re-enactment becomes little more than a game—as it indeed becomes for Joseph.

There is no lack of mythical allusion in the Joseph novels. Joseph descends twice into the pit—first into the well in which his brothers cast him and then into Potiphar's prison; and, as in the cases of Osiris, Tammuz, Dionysus, the pit is symbolic of death and, at the same time, the womb of greater life. The quarrel between Esau and Jacob is seen as a re-enactment of the quarrel between Cain and Abel, and prefigures the quarrel between Joseph and his brothers, just as Jacob's flight from Esau into the land of Laban foreshadows Joseph's journey into Egypt and his service in Potiphar's house. Such allusions and repetitions, however, do not in themselves make the individual case representative in the mythical sense; they do not make the individual case an irreducible mythical type, even if the story itself is based upon mythical material. They do not in themselves ensure a transhuman element in the story, an element necessary to the myth. Indeed, Joseph's participation in God's plans is almost impudent, and God Himself is not a convincingly sacred figure, as seen in Joseph's eyes. When Joseph is travelling with the Ishmaelites, he passes through Hebron from where he would be able to send his father a message. However, he does not contact his father because he sees himself, through association with Tammuz and Osiris, as one who is reborn since his emergence from the well. To honour his new born self he must deny his former self's father. Again, when he hears that the Ishmaelites are procceding towards Egypt, he is sad to imagine his distance from his family but is also joyful because he thinks it appropriate that he should pass from the grave (the well into which his brothers cast him) to the country he has learned to envisage as the kingdom of the dead. Joseph, in short, sees his role as one possible pattern among others. The fact that he has a choice to act or to deviate from that role creates a division between the model and the re-enactment, so that the re-enactment is almost arbitrarily connected to the original model. His faith is the faith of a person who believes in his luck rather than faith in an awesome power. Mann says that Joseph is never completely sad, even when Potiphar sends him to prison, because he sees his circumstances as appropriate to the story; he is confident that this descent will be, according to the mythic pattern, followed by a greater ascent. There is no immediacy, no urgency in his enactment of the myth, and so the pattern becomes not an eternal or elemental drama, but a charm, and his relation to God is highly individualised, as in a fairy tale.

Indeed, the notion of God's participation in the story frequently seems to embarrass Mann. In 'Prelude in the Upper Circles' which opens the fourth volume, Mann adopts the tone of mocking familiarity which Goethe, in his *Faust*, gives to Mephistopheles as he addresses God; but though Faust's trials may be an entertainment for God and the Devil, they are for him deadly earnest, and Joseph's trials lack this force. Mann suggests the working of supernatural influences wryly and grudgingly. When Mont-kaw, the overseer in Potiphar's household who helps Joseph rise in Potiphar's service, first meets Joseph, Mann says:

Perhaps—I will not venture an assertion—perhaps at this moment, upon which so much depended, the planning of the God of his father did a little something extra for Joseph. Perhaps he let fall upon him a light calculated to produce the desired effect upon all beholders. For He, in truth, has given all our senses for pleasure; yet reserved to Himself their use as medium and avenue for His larger purposes to play upon our minds. Hence my suggestion—which, however, I am willing to withdraw if it seems too supernatural an element to be introduced into our very natural tale.

Joseph in Egypt, pp. 125—6

This sophisticated irreverence, however, is completely absent from Mann's treatment of Jacob. This character and his associated themes attain an excellence unsurpassed in any of Mann's works. Jacob's sense of God's power transcends the image of a personable God who grants special individuals special care. His vision of God, which remains steadfast—even strengthened—after Rachel's death, is a vision of dread as well as love. His awareness of God's will is an awareness of a mystery, whereas Joseph stands before God not as before the absolute and immediate, but before a benevolent and familiar consciousness, worthy of the God of *The New English Bible*. Jacob's faith and trust have a kind of resignation which Mann would judge to be more conservative and constricting than Joseph's pragmatic optimism, but Mann shows Jacob's reverence to have a greater profundity. Jacob's re-enactment of the past has an immediacy and sincerity which reveal the past as a mythical present. He is tormented by the idea that he would not be able to obey God's commandment to sacrifice his son as Abraham had been. He is not simply playing with a role, but trying to discover his own worthiness before God, and even in imagination he is more involved in the historical rite than Joseph is in his own trials.

Mann discusses Abraham's willingness to sacrifice his son and Jacob's reluctance to do so along lines similar to Kierkegaard's arguments in *Fear and Trembling*. When Jacob admits to Joseph his fear that his love for his son is greater than his devotion to God, and that he would not be able to meet the demand for such a sacrifice, Joseph replies that Jacob could not perform such a sacrifice not because his love for his son is incompatible with a devotion to God but because he knows such an act would be an abomination in the sight of God. Joseph's sophistication claims knowledge of a moral law which must bind even God's will, whereas, for Jacob, God's will is absolute, and His commandments cannot be set against any standard; His command is the ultimate morality. Kierkegaard, who also uses Abraham's trial to point to the difference between a moral and religious sense of law, sees the absolute commitment to God as an advance in self-realisation over the moral consciousness, but Mann sees such reverence as at least partly superstition. The ego's emancipation from blind obedience is, Mann believes, essential to modern consciousness; he suggests that God truly wills such emancipation for an acceptable, modern God cannot be arbitrarily omnipotent. His point is certainly valid: acceptable morality cannot be based upon arbitrary will, however awesome the source of that will. What makes Joseph's moral knowledge unsatisfactory, however, is that it displaces reverence. Jacob's sense of awe is replaced by Joseph's wit. His knowledge of God's law becomes a supercilious knowledge of God's will, so that Joseph is provided not only with information about how he should behave but also about how God should behave. He knows that God will behave according to mythic patterns, and that after he is 'snatched away' he will be 'lifted up' and, subsequently 'followed after'. He flirts with difficulty, he does not suffer it. His life is his story, as an artist's material is his story, and his detachment is more successful, more assured, more supercilious than that of Aschenbach.

Mann admits that Joseph's confidence is problematic. He says it is an intermediate stage of the emancipation of the ego from archaic reverence. He seeks to show, in the course of the volumes, a progression from egocentricity to collective consciousness. Such a progression is convincingly shown in *Doctor Faustus*, where pride's descent is painful and terrifying, but Joseph's sense of the collective is realised only as an obvious kind of social responsibility which, according to American principles of free enterprise (Mann completed the work in America and saw Joseph's economic measures as a version of Roosevelt's New Deal), is also a means of self-advancement. In *Doctor Faustus* Mann retracts the proposal that knowledge of moral principles gives one a secure grasp upon goodness, for there moral principles fall apart in one's hands—neither the human nor the divine will can be guided by them—and a return to morality can be achieved only through dread and terror.

The Joseph novels begin not with the biblical story but with an investigation of the primal myth. Mann suggests that this myth is the romance of the soul, which he uses to delineate the ultimate tensions in man's soul and which therefore gives a mythical outline to the biblical stories that follow.

The romance of the soul is the story of soul's descent into matter. Once the soul was a substance with independent life which dwelt in simple harmony with God. It had, however, a tremendous longing to mingle with matter and God allowed soul to descend. Matter remained in its sluggish, formless state until God helped soul and matter to join in some semi-permanent form; that is, He created the world. But as He did so, He sent His emissary, spirit, to tell man that the world of base matter was not his rightful place, that there was something higher for which he should strive, that soul—now imprisoned in matter—actually belonged with God. The longer soul remained with matter, however, the more it came to identify itself with matter and with matter's interests. Even the emissary spirit, after spending some time in the world, accepted things as they were and ceased its attempt to achieve a better integration between matter and soul. But man's knowledge that he is both soul and matter brings him disquiet. He must struggle for a better resolution between these elements, even though the final resolution—their divorce—would be his destruction. It is this disquiet, this seeking after a realisation of his higher nature, that led Abraham to seek the Highest One and to bow down only before Him. It is this striving that constitutes the blessing Abraham passed on to Isaac, and which Jacob stole from his brother. Mann believes this tension will be resolved only when the ego is able to stand before God and identify itself with soul. Such an identification, however, involves a struggle with matter—for the reality of man's material aspect cannot be denied, and the overcoming of this human aspect must, in Mann's eyes, be the result of a tumultuous battle—the victor must be susceptible to temptation. Joseph's story is one of worldly success, and therefore it is not to him that the blessing of painful strife is given, but to Judah, the son of Leah (not of the beloved Rachel whose sons are graced with physical loveliness) who is tormented by his own lust and capable of sin and humiliation, as Joseph is not.

It is indeed with such creative but unresolved struggles and bewildered, sensuously perceived spirituality that Mann's imagination comes to life. His portrayal of Jacob is inspirational, and actually does achieve the integration between sense and spirit (not a resolution between them, but an integration of creative rather than destructive tension) before which his imagination was so often defeated. Jacob's immediate connection with his history has a depth and vividness similar to that of the farmers in the opening pages of *The Rainbow*. Lawrence shows the farmers' lives to be permeated by a rich, sensuous awareness of elemental forces and their sense of meaning to be derived from the continuity of their work, from the deep, semiconscious harmony between their work and their world. The blood-sleep of the Marsh farmers is akin to Jacob's heavy, indefinite dreaminess; both indicate an indistinct though deeply felt participation in a transhuman reality. The farmers, however, have their spiritual needs satisfied simply by the symbol of the spire in the distance; their transhuman connection does not involve a yearning towards something higher, whereas Jacob's dreaminess is a struggle to break through the indistinct forces and images. This struggle defines his spirituality, and his spirituality is as immediate to him as the land is to the farmers: to

Jacob it was 'as though the ground beneath his feet were transparent, consisting of crystal layers going down and down without any bottom and lighted by lamps which burned between the layers.'[3] The chords and correspondences which even simple objects wake within his soul blur and fragment his vision. His sensitivity to the world as a manifestation of sacred meaning is keen to the point of painfulness. The image of Jacob's dark, brooding manner, which inspires in observers both respect and an inclination to smile, his groping feelings that rise up without restraint, his frequent physical depression lighted by an influx of spirit—all give his striving an emotional force, and for the first time in Mann, emotion and sensibility feed the spirit.

This rare presentation of emotion as an impetus towards a finer integration of soul and sense has a startling power and excellence. The sexual aspect of the love for Rachel which Jacob transferred, after her death, to her son Joseph, does not introduce a nasty aspect of paternal love, nor does it in any way undermine the tenderness and delicacy of Jacob's paternal passion. The sexual element in his love is not—as it usually is in Mann's other works—a weapon against the spirit or a perversion, but part of the continuity between Jacob's love for the mother and his love for the child. Nor does Jacob's love for Rachel involve the type of passion Mann usually depicts—a passion which destroys the useful and constructive capacities; Jacob's love for Rachel adds to the direction and meaning of his life, and the passion is a tender awareness of her, and a human—not dæmonic—communion. At their first meeting he tells her he is from Beersheba:

> She started and repeated the word, and her mouth, which he had already begun to love, shaped the name of Isaac. His face twitched, his mild eyes ran over. He did not know Laban's people and would not have been eager for contact with them. He was an outlaw, stolen to the lower world, not here of his own will, and felt not much cause for tender feelings. But his nerves gave way; under the strain of the journey they had weakened. He was at his goal, and this maiden, with eyes so darkly sweet, uttered his far-off father's name and was his mother's brother's child.
>
> *Tales of Jacob*, p. 192

Jacob's emotions are part of the total fabric of his life. His capacity for work, for effectiveness, for religious understanding are strengthened rather than threatened by romantic passion. Love, here, involves a grasp upon hope and life; it is an emotion which seeks and finds its realisation in health and normality. Aschenbach's and Hans Castorp's passions thrived amid disease and destruction of their social personalities; their respective passions were at war with respectability and normality because their passions could not survive the commonplace world of daily communication and distraction. Jacob's desire for Rachel, however, is mingled with his desire to work; in fact, to honour his emotion, he knows that he must not think only of his love, but attend to other responsibilities. Nor is Romantic longing, a longing that values its own intensity and pain, the centre of his emotion. Laban insists that Jacob wait seven years before marrying his daughter, but the waiting is not characterised by Tristanesque yearning; rather, it involves an incentive to prove the reality of his feelings, and their reality is confirmed not by his being annihilated by them but by his showing he can live well with them. Sensuous love, the desire for children and the need for a human attachment that provides a sense of human continuity, are happily combined in Jacob's passion.

In Mann's other studies of passion, the concern for goodness is shown to be either waylaid or distorted, but in Jacob's case the need to value one's emotions is shown to be as strong as passion itself. Here emotions have some sense of measure; they are governed by one's values, and bound up with one's deepest values. The story of Laban's deception when, on Jacob's wedding night, the father replaces Rachel with his older daughter Leah, and the subsequent shattering of Jacob's faith in the capacity of his sense, to honour his spirit, is fully ironic, but it is nonetheless clear that Laban's trick is a desecration. Though Jacob's sensuality is cruelly mocked, its value is not denied. Laban's deception shows that emotion can be misguided by pleasure, but it can be misguided not because its sense of value is fraudulent but because emotion is human, and anything human can be desecrated. It is not an easy lesson, however, and this tale of his spirit's blindness while his senses have their utmost satisfaction is, of all the tales that had written themselves in the lines of his face, most present to Jacob during his musing:

As his seeing hands left her face and found her body and the the skin of her body, Ishtar pierced them both to the marrow, the bull of heaven breathed and its breath was as the breath of both that mingled. And all that windy night did Jacob find the child of Laban a glorious mate, great in delights and mighty to conceive, and she received him many times and again and again, so that they counted no more but the shepherds answered one another that it was nine times.

Tales of Jacob, p. 253

The vulgar comedy of the shepherds keeping track of Jacob's prowess and the emphasis upon his unqualified enjoyment does not deny the reality of his need to connect this pleasure to Rachel, and to his love for her. Laban's inability to understand Joseph's despair upon the discovery that his bride was Leah, points, by its very bluntness, to Jacob's finer and more subtle consciousness. Laban mocks him: is his manhood exhausted after one night with Leah? He cannot understand that the wedding-night consummation had a significance for Jacob that cannot be recaptured, and that Jacob's concern is for the proper meaning of his desire, not for his sexual potency. Laban, the man of earth alone, cannot understand the spirit's faith, nor its horror at discovering its own frailty.

The tension of sensuality—of sensuality as an impediment to good action and good feeling—is always present among the people of Jacob's camp. Sometimes this tension is presented in farce, as when Sichem's people are all circumcised to placate Jacob for the theft of his daughter Dinah, and then, on the third day after the mass circumcision, when the wound is known to be at its worst, Jacob's sons attack the city. Sometimes the farce is eclipsed by pity, as when Reuben, angry with his father for neglecting his mother Leah in favour of the maid Billah, seduces Billah himself, and the maid bows down before Jacob, scratching the breasts which Reuben had confused and aroused and which could never again belong to the man she loved. But however much sensuality confuses the spirit, it is not divorced from spirit. Jacob's union with God, confirmed by circumcision, is a sensuous, passionate attachment. The God of Jacob is jealous, too, in an almost sexual manner, for, in response to Jacob's love for Rachel, He makes her barren while Leah, unloved, is fertile. Communion with God is passionate and immediate; the dream which Jacob wrestles to claim the name 'Israel' is a

frightful, heavy, sensual dream, yet with a certain wild sweetness; no light and fleeting vision that passes and is gone, but a dream of such physical warmth, so dense with actuality, that it left a double legacy of life behind it as the tides leave the fruits of the sea on the strand at the ebb.

Tales of Jacob, p. 85

In this struggle which wins him the name means 'fighter for God' Jacob is wounded in the hollow of the thigh: contact with God always leaves some physical mark, with sexual overtones, as a pledge.

This reverence, submerged in sensuality, is lost in Joseph's wry view of religious influences. His dreams, too, lack the dynamism and awe of Jacob's dreams. When Joseph tells Benjamin how he dreamed of being lifted by an eagle and carried over the earth, the younger brother asks whether he was not terrified, and Joseph answers, 'Why should I tremble at my own dream?' Joseph's dreams are modern and secular; they are psychological rather than religious. They can more easily be construed as wish fulfilments than as messages from God. They are from God only in the very loose sense that the Hebrews' God is a God with a promise, and that these dreams prepare Joseph for his promised future, by making Joseph recognise his own ambition and by rousing his brothers to such fury that they force Joseph on the tortuous path to his success. It is Joseph's faith in his dreams of supremacy, not their divine reality, that makes them prophetic. Joseph's treatment of the Pharaoh's dreams, too, is Freudian rather than religious. Like Freud, Joseph maintains that the dreamer and interpreter are one, and the Pharaoh's dreams are prophetic as expressions of fear. It is not merely court etiquette but sound psychology when Joseph says that in interpreting the Pharaoh's dreams (which he does according to free association with the dream-images) he is only telling the Pharaoh what he already knows.

The more individual, psychological aspect of Joseph's dreams represents, for Mann, the emancipation of the ego from Jacob's fierce attachment to a God who dominates his consciousness. This emancipation will allow greater freedom to the individual, and greater possibility of development. This individual freedom, however, as represented by Joseph, shows a detachment and pride that makes the greater sophistication seem a loss rather than a gain. Joseph's individualism and Mann's mythical allusions do not mix well. Joseph uses myth to enhance the importance of his individual case; myth seems to be reduced to psychology. But the power of the myth depends upon the characters being vehicles for supraconscious forces. Repeatedly Joseph likens himself to Tammuz and Adonis, but Joseph himself is the artist who depicts similarities, and his attention is on the play of allusion rather than the immediate reality and the powerful associations that reveal its meaning. Jacob's more archaic consciousness is also more profound. Upon *Genesis* 37:35 ('And all his sons and all his daughters rose up to comfort him; but he refused to be comforted; and he said, For I will go down to the grave unto my son mourning. Thus his father wept for him') Mann places the mythical story of the descent of Tammuz's mother to her son's grave. Jacob seizes this story, and his grief becomes an aspiration to become God Himself and recreate his son:

[. . .] I would kneel down and enclose in my arms the clay and kiss it as I could kiss it, from the bottom of my heart [. . .] There! he shrieked aloud. Eliezer, lo! 'The body turns red, red as fire, it glows, it scorches me, but I do not let it down. I hold it fast in my arms and kiss it again. Then it is extinguished and water flows into the clay body, it swells and gushes with water, and lo, hair springs up on his head, and nails grow on his fingers and toes. Then I kiss him for the third time and blow into him my breath which is God's breath; and fire and water and breath of air, these three bring it out that the fourth, the earth, wakens to life and in deep amazement opens its eyes to me the awakener and speaks, 'Abba, dear Father'.

Young Joseph, p. 235

From this type of passionate vision Joseph is liberated. He trusts his wit and the benign pattern of the myth while his father struggles to discover the myth's purpose and meaning. Jacob's visions and sentiments are re-enactments of eternally human and suprahuman forces. As such they have the poetic power of myth. Joseph's visions and sentiments are those of an individual—a mere individual—who likes to describe himself in mythical terms. Joseph's emancipation is modern, but in its modernity it exhibits the poverty of the purely secular consciousness.

Though Jacob's concreteness and dense allusiveness do not recur elsewhere in these volumes, the power of his image has reverberations in other characters. Indeed, the dominant character type in the Joseph novels is that of the father, mirroring, in various ways, the presence of God the Father. Potiphar, whose fleshy form is like that of Reuben (who protected Joseph from the angry assault of his other brothers), is the paternal judge and chastiser. His vulnerability, owing to his sexual impotence, creates possibilities of fear and vengefulness, but temperance and affection rule his judgement in the end. The sorrowful patience and weary but dignified loneliness he exhibits as he speaks to Mut the accuser, reflect the father-image as a loving but chastening judge whose justice isolates him from the human arena:

'Patience!' he answered her as softly, bending down from his seat. 'For here will each in his turn have justice and judgement, and his guilt will overtake the culprit. Sit quietly! You will soon be able to arise from your sitting as satisfied as though you yourself had been judge. I judge for you—though without admixture of all too human feeling—and you may rejoice! For were feeling and its violence to pronounce the judgement, there might be no end of remorse.'

After he had so whispered to her he sat up straight again and spoke:

'Take courage in your hands, Osariph, my former steward, for now I come to you, and you too shall hear my judgement [. . .]'

Joseph in Egypt, p. 481

Mont-kaw the overseer, on the other hand, bears the aspect of the indulgent father who plans for his son's worldly advancement and gladly sacrifices his own position to his son's. Judah, again, becomes the father-brother protector as he pleads for mercy on Benjamin's behalf when the silver cup is discovered among his belongings.

The father image is central to the drama of these tales. It is from paternal favour that Joseph derives both his sense of purpose and his pride and this pride, in turn, must be tempered by paternal chastisement. Then, it is Joseph in the role of the father, as he appears to the young Pharaoh, and then as he provides for the people, that constitutes the success story. This father type, however, which is finely achieved elsewhere, fails when Joseph himself assumes the role. The favour of the young Pharaoh is essential to Joseph's success, yet Mann does not offer a vivid account of the relationship. A good psychological story might have been told: the Pharaoh is fatherless and dominated by his mother; this, combined with his uncertainty as ruler, could lay the foundation for a creative dependence upon the older, very handsome man who interprets his disturbing dreams and advises him. Nonetheless, Mann tells the story of the Pharaoh's favour as though it were a question of royal whim (like Goethe, Mann was interested in the notion of luck, or the whim of God's favour, in the allocation of position and talent, and in the moral value so often attached to amoral but God-given assets such as beauty, wealth and sensibility). This final episode in Joseph's advancement, therefore, is neither psychologically or poetically necessary, but merely fortuitous.

The women characters, as types, are far more limited than the male types. The women's connection to the blessing of spiritual aspiration can be made only by bearing a son who will partake in the blessing. Their struggles, therefore, are not on behalf of a better integration of their own impulses but for men's love and fertility. Again Mann's world of human desire becomes, in the feminine sphere, a world in which sex is prone to wage a nasty battle against the spirit and the social self. Rachel and Leah are safe because, as ordinary women, their social selves are at one with their sexual selves. It is in his study of Potiphar's wife Mut that Mann presents a woman who is something other than wife and breeder. This vital, passionate woman is Aschenbach's counterpart. Ignorance and the need to deny her own impulses make her destructive; but she, in the guise of woman the seductress, is more powerful than Aschenbach, and her destructive will is more aggressive.

When Mut's parents gave her to Potiphar she was a child, blithe, merry and free: 'She was like a water-flower swimming upon a glassy pool, smiling beneath the kisses of the sun, untouched by the knowledge that its long stem is rooted in the black slime of the depth'.[4] Her happiness depended upon ignorance of the source of her deepest impulses. Her infatuation with Joseph is a violent outburst against the suppression of this slime-root; but though the analysis of her behaviour as outrage against unfair suppression goes some way towards forgiving Mut her behaviour, it condemns the instinct which drives her. The deepest source of her impulses is unqualifiably destructive and stagnant. Only a controlled drainage of such impulses could save her: a wise society allows such impulses a functional place, but in themselves they are deadly to society and to the spirit. As in Aschenbach's case, suppression strengthens these impulses, and her sexuality destroys the spiritual pride which (like Aschenbach's proud discipline) is based upon a fragile network of values. She is the priestess of an outworn religion; her god is without a promise and without a future. Her passion, like that of Hans Castorp, is based upon the despair that dwells within an empty society. Her passion is a will to destroy the social fabric and her own exalted position in it. Her passion has its own laws, and will fight to preserve them:

> To delude oneself, up to the point at which it is too late to turn back—that one must do at all costs. To be awakened, warned, called back to oneself before it is too late: therein lies the danger which is at all costs to be avoided.
>
> *Joseph in Egypt*, p. 292

This, obviously, is a return to the frenzied atmosphere of disease-
ridden Venice and the Berghof Sanatorium in which ecstasy and
destruction appear to the passionate person as the highest goods.
Mut's evil, however, also extends to the possibility of organised
violence. She must accuse Joseph, because he is the occasion of the
eruption of her own sexual feelings; she must accuse him to convince
herself and everyone else that he is at fault. She addresses her audience
as 'Egyptian brothers' and rouses them against the foreigner who has
invaded their home. She needs a scapegoat for the frustration and
shame of her own violent feelings. Thus Mann identifies as a political
counterpart of passion (in other words, destructive and self-
destructive impulses) the highly organised barbarism of the Nazis.
The primitive roots of life, when celebrated in the political sphere,
become organised aggression and far more dangerous than a personal,
wayward decadence.

Mut's tragedy arises within the confusions of Egypt's religion.
Mann sets the last part of Joseph's story in the reign of Akenhaten,
who ruled from 1369 BC to 1352 BC and who was known as the
heretic Pharaoh. He worshipped one god, the Sun-Disc Aten, a god
with a more benevolent aspect than that of the traditional Amun-Re.
Mann represents the traditional god as a dark, fecund force with
a sensuality that enervates the spirit but also demands that his
worshippers sacrifice their sexuality. The sacrifice of Potiphar's
potency was made by his parents who, as brother and sister, were
themselves fertile according to the laws of the earth's deep, stagnant
darkness, not according to the laws of the sun and the new order.
Sensing their lack of harmony with the new face of religion, they
hoped to placate the god of light by offering to him their son's
sexuality. Mut, as Amun's priestess, as the guardian of the old order
and of primitive, rank fecundity, must have her revenge.

Mann, therefore, bases his explanation of a Romantically conceived eruption of chaos and instinct upon Egypt's religious history.
In spite of his careful scholarship there is generally something
patronising in his treatment of Egyptian culture. The descriptions of
the various religions Joseph encounters on his travels through Egypt
are highly coloured by Mann's own conception of corruption, and his
criticism of these religions, or his analysis of their stagnation, is not
well balanced. Mann sees the worship of an animal-god not only as a
primitive religion but also as worship of the primitive, that is,
worship of instinct and sexuality—and, in Mann's view, instinct and
sexuality are stagnant and destructive; paradoxically, he sees fertility

cults as constricting growth and rejuvenation. The city of On enjoys a greater liberalism, but its god is shallow; the city itself shines with an overbright gold and inflames the eyelids, for such an untarnished view of life is blind and ignorant. The people of Menfe, aware that their god is outmoded, adopt a jesting manner, a manner which stems from a nihilistic spirit—just as, in *Doctor Faustus*, Leverkühn's parodistic style arises from a disbelief in the forms it employs.

Naturally Mann must use Egyptian material for his own purposes. He is not writing a history of Egyptian religion and culture. Nevertheless, the simple schematic use of his material is often unsatisfactory. The historical accuracy of *Anthony and Cleopatra* is irrelevant; what is important is that Shakespeare creates from an Egyptian atmosphere, a rich and consistent poetic world in which psychology and image and morality complement one another and justify one another. Mann, however, moulds his material too tightly into his schema, and there is no poetic investigation of his material. When he offers detailed descriptions of the setting, his treatment has an aimless extravagance worthy of a Hollywood spectacular:

> The side walls were covered with paintings unlike anything elsewhere in the country; strange peoples and customs were depicted; obviously there were landscapes from the islands of the sea. Women in gay stiff clothing sat or moved about, their bosoms bare in the tight bodices, their hair curling above the ribbon on their foreheads and falling on their shoulders in long plaits. Pages attended them, in strange elaborate costume, and handed drink from tapering jugs. A little prince with a wasp waist, particoloured trousers and lambskin boots, a coronet with a gay gush of feathers on his curly head, strutted complacently between rankly blossoming grasses and shot with his bow and arrow at fleeting game which leaped away with all four hooves clear of the ground. Acrobats turned somersaults over the backs of raging bulls for the diversion of ladies and gentlemen looking down from the balconies.
>
> *Joseph the Provider*, p. 125

There is no attempt here to investigate the living culture which lies behind the scene. To describe the bull leaping as a diversion is to ignore the power and grace of such performances (at least as such practices are depicted in Egyptian art); and though such palaces did undoubtedly reveal a decadent culture, Mann's presentation indicates an almost complacent judgement of the culture: he is dutifully delineating all scenes in the palace, and each one seen is equally and totally a sign of decadence.

Mann's use of Egyptian myth also has the simplicity of preconception. The contrast between the dead religion of old Egypt and the rejuvenation supported by Joseph and Akenhaten is over-precise. The old religion, as Mann presents it, is totally dead; indeed, its death and sexuality have none of the poetic vitality of Aschenbach's sensual decadence. Nor does Mann fairly represent the subtlety of the myth's identification of death and sexuality; nor does he describe the myth from which the identification arose. According to the Egyptian tale, Secknet the slayer was sent out by Ra to destroy the evil that had arisen among men, but in killing people she developed a taste for blood and she began to kill without discretion, good and bad alike, until Ra made her drunk and changed her, by renaming her, into Hathor, the lady of love. The identification between death and sexuality, then, was, according to Egyptian myth, a resolution of the problem of the will to destruction. Love is seen as a means of taming the will, whereas Mann, with his view of love as a version rather than transformation of destruction and death impulses, saw the identification as sheer, wilful corruption.

When Mann's interest in scenic description, however, is with the emotional or psychological story, his images are finely atmospheric and suggestive. The scene in which Mut begs her husband to dismiss Joseph (when she first realises her passion for him and in trying to overcome it) marvellously combines the visual aspect of her ritual-like approach with the disturbing emotional currents. Potiphar is sitting in the western hall with the declining light glowing round him. A black shadow falls upon one of the pillars as Mut's handmaiden crouches like a tiger in her subservience, asking permission for Mut to approach him. As Mut leaves, having had her request denied, she leans against the pillar, lowering her head to hide her excitement and joy. The characters are seen to move about the palace constrained by protocol, yet use their restraint (crouching like a tiger in subservience) to express their corrupt will, while their will predominates despite the restraint. The descriptions of Joseph's travels, too, are frequently described with a fine, epic quality revealed both in the slow, expansive rhythm of the language that measures the continuous toil of the Ishmaelites' journey and in the images which combine natural descriptions with Joseph's alienation. The desert is like a country damned, like the illimitable floor of the sea, shutting them in with the corpse-coloured sand up to the hot bleached horizon. Across the plain the heat vibrations looked as though near to bursting into tongues of flame, and sand whirled in the air so that men wrapped their heads before this evil dance of death and tried not to look, but rode blindly past these horrors.

Joseph in Egypt, p. 55

The deathly aspect here is enforced by images which capture a poetic reality in the desert, which Mann fails to capture in his treatment of Egyptian culture and religion.

In his essay on Fontane, Mann says that myth and psychology are essentially opposed to one another: myth belongs to the poet, who conserves it, whereas psychology undermines and reduces the myth for the sake of enlightenment. In the Joseph novels Mann attempts to combine myth and psychology. The results are extremely uneven. The power of the myth resides in the image, which must speak for itself and therefore it must speak with an open-endedness and incompleteness for which Mann's novelist's and historian's approach can rarely allow. The volumes contain a story too detailed and therefore too individualised to present a mythical mode of thought. The critical, psychological technique used for every character other than Jacob can only present a personal tale. Joseph acts on behalf of mankind, and he modifies his egoism to serve the people, but his ego is not bound by those primitive forces that would make his story truly representative of a mythical story. Mann has not yet found a creative resolution for the morally problematic energies and imagination.

7 Mann and Goethe

Mann's admiration for Nietzsche and Wagner was modified by his distrust for their respective promotions of the deepest human energies, in their natural, precivilised form. Nietzsche's portrait of the hero as a man who joyfully accepted, for all eternity, a suffering life, and his conception of the best life as a life in which pain and strife were cultivated, seemed to Mann one of those facets of Romanticism which the humanist must reject. Nietzsche may have nobly rejected Wagner on behalf of life, but Mann understood that the death wish in Wagner's works is based upon a celebration of the same energies Nietzsche valued. Indeed, Wagner's death longing is not a desire to escape these elemental, gigantic energies but to escape the world which constrains them; it is a longing to dwell forever in a state of glorified intensity. Both Nietzsche and Wagner share the Romanticist's refusal to compromise: Nietzsche suggests an eternal battle against compromising influences; Wagner's music, generally, creates a world in which compromise does not exist.

Goethe was equally a child of nature. His imagination had an equally powerful grasp of elemental energy and a sympathy with the wild exuberance of Romanticism. He was nevertheless, according to Mann, able to achieve a delicate and dextrous style that balances the dæmonic and the urbane, the lyrical and the psychological, mystery and clarity. Goethe disliked Romanticism's love for pain and its respect for instinct. He was interested in the promotion of man's happiness and health, not in the realisation of his dæmonic strength. He believed that pain was worthwhile only in so far as it led to enlightenment and courage. And Mann saw Goethe's criticism of Romanticism as a renunciation of his own elemental, energetic, perilous imagination.

Though it is true that in his later works Goethe modified the emotional storms of *The Sufferings of Young Werther*, in which intensity and anguish are glorified, the modification is a development rather than a rejection. In Goethe's best works the wild exuberance of Romanticism remains strong. Mann cites *Elective*

Affinities as an example of Goethe's ability to combine the finest parts of Logos and Eros. [1] He sees this novel as a splendid reconciliation of emotion and morality, with the moral aspect emerging from the psychological. The combination of emotion and morality in the novel, however, is static and contrived. The respective couples' passion is bred within and thrives upon indulgence and boredom, yet it lacks the disturbing force of Hans Castorp's (similarly bred) passion. The impasse of the couples' passion is resolved only by Ottilie starving herself to death, and the reconciliation of morality with passion is a torturous self-denial by all concerned, and the good of their ultimately 'correct' behaviour is highly obscure. Indeed, Goethe at his worst could be precisely what Mann describes—a writer who ignores the more disturbing and recalcitrant aspects of emotion on the basis of moral theory. This policy cannot achieve a creative resolution; it merely diminishes the imagination's grasp of nature.

At his best, however, Goethe employs the full force of his vision of natural, elemental energy. In *Faust* vitality combines with human value, even as the vitality is a boundless and tormenting urge:

> Des Lebens Pulse schlagen frisch lebendig,
> Ätherische Dämmerung milde zu begrüßen;
> Du, Erde, warst auch diese Nacht beständig
> Und atmest neu erquickt zu meinen Füßen,
> Beginnest schon, mit Lust mich zu umgeben,
> Du regst und rührst ein kräftiges Beschließen,
> Zum höchsten Dasein immerfort zu streben. –
>
> Part 2, Act 1, lines 4679–85

(Life's pulses waken refreshed to greet the mild dawn's ethereal vision. You, earth, have also withstood this night, and breath with new life beneath my feet and begin by surrounding me with pleasure, and command a strong resolution—to strive for the highest being with all my powers.)

At his best, Goethe does not tame his elemental sympathies, but ties the darker forces to human aspirations. He shows longing springing up from dark sources and reaching towards the light.

Nature contains the tension between the spirit and the senses but, in *Faust*, it does not mark the division between spirit and sense. Faust's soliloquy, 'Erhabner Geist, du gabst mir gabst mir alles', (Part One, lines 3217–50) expresses gratitude for his ability to enjoy nature, not coldly and reflectively, but with a passion that penetrates deep into nature's heart. Mephistopheles then mocks Faust's apparently spiritual penetration by exploiting the obviously sexual imagery. How delightful it must be, Mephistopheles jeers, to embrace the earth and, enraptured in one's own ecstasy, approach godliness, so that one's love of nature becomes a spiritual orgasm. The point of Mephistopheles' derision is based upon Faust's previous seduction of Margarete; it is a reminder that his sensuous appreciation of life is out of control, and that it resulted in the destruction of a young girl. This lack of control is the devil's doing; it is Mephistopheles who lights a wild fire in Faust's breast that pushes him from desire to enjoyment and then, in enjoyment, makes him long for desire. It is this insatiable longing in which longing itself is desired that confuses the spirit; and it is this heaven-storming longing which Goethe distrusted in Romanticism; but it is not a longing that shows—as Mephistopheles (and sometimes Mann) would have it—that the spiritual aspect of longing is fraudulent. Faust demands:

> Was bin ich denn, wenn es nicht möglich ist,
> Der Menschheit Krone zu erringen,
> Nach der sich alle Sinne dringen?

                                        Part 1, lines 1803–4

(What am I then, if I cannot reach for mankind's crown, which all the senses crave?)

The human senses themselves yearn for the highest spiritual fulfilment; the senses can be distorted and confused, as Mephistopheles confuses them, but their proper object is a fulfilment far more profound than gratification. It is indeed such a perfect mingling of the sensuous and spiritual in Wagner's works that makes nonsense of the notion that the composer is either a voluptuary or a barbarian.

Goethe did not need to renounce his sympathy with the extreme and gigantic in nature to establish a moral concern. His portrayal of Faust's energies exposes their dangers but does not reject them. His heaven and hell-storming were always human explorations, and his interest in man's aspirations was tied to his interest in man's capacities and needs. The vividness of Faust's pursuit and the vagueness of its object are characteristic of Mann's Romanticism, too; but Goethe's notion of the inexhaustible, alluring force (what he calls the eternal feminine) leads one forward, not, as in Mann, to destruction. In Goethe's works imagination is a positive force; it is directed not against but creatively upon the world. The imagination does not turn away from the world and isolate one from it, as Mann shows it to do;

the imagination transforms the world into its own gigantic image. Imagination makes one hungry for life; the longing that accompanies imagination is a longing for life. Mann's view of the resolution of imagination's burden in death and stasis is, in effect, the impasse that will allow Mephistopheles to claim Faust; for when Faust no longer has the urge to act, when he ceases to strive, he is in the devil's power. And though Mann agrees with this dæmonic assessment of statis, he sees stasis as a dæmonic temptation, too, and as the primary trend of the imagination. His inability to see life involvement as a genuine outgrowth of imagination, his own inability to portray an imagin-ation that craves integration with reality, leads to the mistaken view that in his best work Goethe renounced the strength of his own imagination for the sake of moral principle.

Mann's attachment to life, quite simply, is not very strong. His strength lies in his understanding of the fascinations that paralyse life-interest, in the passions that destroy practical interests and the social personality, in his sense of rich mystery and satisfaction of stasis and release. His Nirvana sympathies colour his view of the artist, too, for art is a means of turning away from life. The talent for literature, the poet in *Royal Highness* tells Klaus Heinrich, consists in an inability to cope with life. However painful Tonio Kröger believes his sacrifice of life to art to be, it is a sacrifice which is in accord with the artist's inclinations. The artist's personality is not one that desires life; he does not actually renounce something he might have had, or something he would like to have.

Mann's fictional study of Goethe, *Lotte in Weimar*, is an in-vestigation of the way an artist affects people close to him. It is a study of an artist's use of people for the sake of his art. The emphasis is no longer, as in *Tonio Kröger*, on the artist's loneliness, but on the demands the artist makes upon other people and his ultimate indifference to other people, for they are only so much paper on which to write. Mann did not create Goethe exactly in his own image, but much of his portrait is, while based upon material from Goethe's writings and upon the writings of Goethe's associates, highly influenced by the pictures of the artist Mann draws elsewhere. Goethe told Eckermann that he was surprised how much life he was able to portray in his youthful works, despite his inexperience; but though Goethe believed that a poet's knowledge of human nature is in some sense innate (in that one aspect of a character will lead a poet to the discovery of other aspects, even without observation) knowledge of customs and social behaviour must be learned through observation. Goethe is pleased by how much he had done with such little experience, but he in no way supposes, as did Mann's poet in *Royal Highness*, that inexperience is the seedbed of creativeness. It is not that Mann saw the artist as, necessarily, a recluse. His isolation and inexperience are a matter of emotional detachment rather than actual withdrawal from society. Zeitblom compares Leverkühn's emotional absence to an abyss into which the emotions people offered him fall silent, without a trace. Klaus Heinrich, the royal counterpart of the artist, whose life is devoted to the creation of illusion, is suspected by Imma of emotional emptiness, and Aschenbach's emotional detachment finally destroys him. In *Lotte in Weimar*, however, the artist abounds with emotions. His ultimate coldness and detachment arise from the artistic purpose of these emotions; they are, essentially, unreal.

Lotte in Weimar is drawn around Charlotte Kestner's visit to Weimar forty-four years after the summer Goethe spent with her and her fiancé. During that summer Goethe had absorbed the material for *The Sufferings of Young Werther*. Even after the publication of the first part of *Faust* Goethe's fame was centred upon this early novel. Werther had become a cult figure. People dressed as the character had been said to dress. It was even fashionable to commit suicide through the despair of unrequited love, as Goethe's Werther did. Charlotte was well known to have been the model of Werther's Lotte, and her visit, in Mann's novel, is her attempt to come to terms with her position as the fictional Lotte. Now that the active business of her life is completed (her children are grown and her husband is dead), now that the reality which had saved her from the youthful Goethe is less demanding, she comes to the poet's home to explore the possible, the intense and intriguing, the Romantic world she rejected on behalf of normal, wholesome life. She is fascinated by this possible world, but she realises that she was never actually in danger of succumbing to it. The kiss that Goethe had snatched from her as they were picking strawberries had, as most of the events of that summer, been repainted in the vivid and glowing colours of the novel; and even though that awkward, actual kiss had been nothing like the turbulent kisses Werther lavishes upon Lotte, Charlotte had felt it as a mad, melancholic kiss. She had resisted Goethe's passion not only through love and loyalty to Kestner, but through fear of the world from which that kiss had come. She feared something in the nature of that turbulent, vagabond prince-poet, something mysterious, irresponsible—and unreal. Goethe's emotions are investigations of life, investigations made for the sake of his art. Once the poet has enough material, he is finished with the emotion and with the person who provided the occasion for the emotion. Riemer, Goethe's secretary, explains to the Weimar visitor that such irresponsibility and wildness are necessary to artistic objectivity. The gaze of absolute art, he tells Charlotte, is both absolute love and absolute nihilism and indifference; poetic genius is this combination of the godlike and the diabolic.

The artist's coldness and indifference are in fact one aspect of his boundless sympathies. For a passionate appreciation of all natural things involves respect for good and evil alike, and therefore involves nihilism. It is interesting that Mann focuses upon this remark of Riemer, for it both points to Goethe's excellence and to an essential difference between Goethe's irony and Mann's. Speaking to Eckermann of *Wilhelm Meister* (January 18 1825) Goethe said that it was not right for people to seek a central point in the work. 'I should think a rich manifold life, brought close to our eyes, would be enough without any express tendency,' he said. Indeed, the good and evil in his characters and in the situations they face arise from a rich manifold nature, and the ironic amalgamation of good and evil does not reduce or confuse the value of any element. Mann's irony takes the form: 'this is desirable, but what makes it desirable is its evil', or, 'this is good, but its goodness will lead to evil'. The trust and warm abandon Margarete feels in Faust's arms is not something which is desirable because it is destructive, nor is it something which in itself (like Aschenbach's passion) becomes corrupt; Margarete's love has a value that is not undermined by its disastrous consequences. To Mann such sympathy appeared nihilistic, yet his own rigorously moral approach to the desirable and the beautiful leads to a greater nihilism, for it denies that human good can be measured or detected by human desires. This is the impasse upon which Mann's irony turns.

A further diabolic aspect of Goethe's godliness, as presented in *Lotte in Weimar*, is the boundless sympathy that is essentially impersonal. Sympathy with all people and all forms of life renders individual connections unimportant. Goethe is like Don Giovanni in his love for women as a love for loveliness and delicacy and tenderness and goodness they represent, or for the female image rather than for the individual woman. Mann successfully conveys the image of the Olympian Goethe (a much less tame Goethe and much less prone to noble renunciation than the Goethe who appears in Mann's essays) whose passion is a shortlived whirlwind, both seductive and destructive. Charlotte sees that Goethe's passion for her was a kind of play, and an emotional means to an end that was unreal and transhuman—she sees that his passion was a means to his art. This understanding actually increases her resentment, however, for as a young woman she was forced to take him seriously. Charlotte had to employ all her energy to struggle back to life, and she knows that other women, who had been similarly used, have simply pined away when the vagabond prince left them. She resents him more than she would a lover who simply happened to be faithless; she resents the seductive force of his passion which is forceful and seductive and mysterious and intriguing because it is a transhuman, almost impersonal emotion and could never be constant.

Mann's view is that Goethe used life for the sake of his art, but this description of the poet's behaviour ignores his concern for the life— the person—behind the art work. Eckermann reports Goethe as saying, 'But of what use are all the arts of a talent, if we do not find in a theatrical piece an amiable or great personality in the author?'[2] Goethe's respect for reality was certainly bound up with his respect for art, but his creativeness stems from his interest in reality, not vice versa. He said

All my poems are occasioned poems, suggested by real life, and having therein a firm foundation. I attach no value to poem snatched out of the air.

Let none say that reality wants poetical interest; for in this the poet proves his vocation, that he has the art to win from a common subject an interesting side. Reality must give the motive, the points to be expressed—the kernel; but to work out of it a beautiful animated whole, belongs to the poet.[3]

Goethe himself, therefore, would not agree with Mann's portrayal of the artist whose interest was art alone and who found no real satisfaction in life; nor is it likely that Goethe would have accepted Mann's analysis of the poet's personal behaviour as a means to his art. Nevertheless, the artist is not always a reliable spokesman for his own psychology, and Goethe's extravagant passions are plausibly interpreted by Mann. But this analysis of the poet's general motivation is only part of Mann's moral tale.

Charlotte's oppression by this whirlwind world of poetry, her struggle to hold onto her own normal, active life, are shared by all people close to Goethe. Goethe as a poet both enthralls people by representing the world of imagination, and uses them for the sake of his art. As Charlotte watches Goethe at lunch and listens to the laughter of the people round him,

> it seemed to her for one dreadful moment that the loud and general laughter of these devotees was meant to cover up and drown out something else, something the more uncanny in that it was like a personal threat to her very self, while at the same time it concealed an invitation to share it and be one of them.[4]

The atmosphere around Goethe, Charlotte feels, smells of human sacrifice. All the people she meets in Weimar, all those who have sought her out, try to resolve—as she is trying to do on this visit—their personal lives with their places in the lives of the poet. Riemer, Goethe's private secretary, cannot fulfil his lifelong ambition to obtain a university post; when offered such a position he cannot accept it because he cannot leave Weimar and Goethe. August, Goethe's son, is so bound up with his role as the famous man's son that he borrows all his thoughts from his father. Just as Zeitblom who, in his devotion to the composer, considers his own personal life as an aside, the family and devotees of Goethe are too timid to live according to their own impulses and interests, for these seem petty in contrast to those of the poet.

Mann presents these cases of self-denial as cases for which the artist is responsible. And Mann's Goethe accepts this responsibility. In Charlotte's final conversation with Goethe (which might be Charlotte's hallucination, but which nonetheless articulates the problem of the artist's relation to his characters and to the people upon whom the characters are based) he asks her to forgive him for the use to which he has put her. He tells her it should be sufficient that he gave her eternal youth in his art. Indeed, as an artist he believes that art compensates for all. He defends himself against the charge that he demands sacrifices of others by saying that he, too, is sacrificed to his art. This admission is a poor excuse, however, for though he does sacrifice his personal life, this is a loss felt only by the people close to him. His Olympian stature is undiminished by the sacrifice.

There are several moral strands within the theme of the artist *vis-à-vis* his characters and friends. First, there is the question of the use the artist makes in his work of his friends' private lives. Here there is a possibility of embarrassing them and betraying what was supposed to be confidential. This is simply a question of good manners and discretion. It is in no way peculiar to the artist, and it is a falsely posed moral question to ask whether the artist has a right to make use of his acquaintances or whether his works justifies their embarrassment. An artist may or may not be well-mannered and considerate; but this question is independent of the question of the value of the artist's works. If he is a great artist he may nonetheless be ill-mannered, and the question of his greatness in no way mitigates his personal behaviour. The second problem involved in Charlotte's sense of a sacrificial atmosphere surrounding Goethe, is the power of the poet's personality and its limiting effect on the people close to him. These people, however, are inhibited and bound to Goethe through their own meagre natures. When Charlotte tells Goethe that it is people's own duty to be resolute, to make themselves their own ends even though they are means for the artist, she seems to be resisting her own tendency to blame the poet—and this blame is endorsed by the poet's image of himself as the sacrificial flame, which both attracts and destroys the moth. Nevertheless, her remark is, without qualification, true. Greatness—as artistic excellence—is not responsible for the daunting effect it has upon other people. Goethe cannot be blamed either for Riemer's attachment or his son's mimicry. When a person's life is cramped by another's greatness his plight may be pathetic and his battle worthy of sympathy, but it is a poor argument to say that greatness is at fault for others' discomfort with their own mediocrity.

The more interesting problem concerns the artist's sincerity and the motives of his passions. The artist's use of other people can be judged as any other person's use of other people; but each case has its own story, and the artist's story might well reveal an artist's motive. There are two possibilities in the type of phenomenon Mann describes in *Lotte in Weimar*: the artist might instigate emotional situations which will act as a creative stimulus or, alternatively, the problematic emotional situations the artist finds himself in are solved not by his personality but by his art. In the first case, the artist's emotions might indeed be real, but the reality is, paradoxically, manufactured for the sake of art; only if the emotions are real can they provide authentic artistic material. It is such ambiguous sincerity which intrigued Mann and which he explored so magnificently in his final novel, *Felix Krull*. Goethe, however, seems to exhibit the second type of artistic personality. His art is an overflow of life appreciation and an attempt to resolve problems that arose within his life. In *Doctor Faustus* Mann portrayed an artist whose work mirrored life's problems, but he was blind to the possibility of art arising from an attachment to life.

8 The Nihilistic Face of Aestheticism

Confessions of Felix Krull, Confidence Man is a study of a life dominated by imagination. It is the story of an artist, the subject of whose art is his own life. In Mann's view the artist's primary aims are illusion and entertainment and, therefore, his use of truth is only secondary; the artist is truthful only when reality can be used as a means of captivating his audience:

> To the artist, new experiences of 'truth' are new incentives to the game, new possibilities of expression, no more. He believes in them, he takes them seriously, just so far as he needs, in order to give them the fullest and most profound expression. In all that he is serious, serious even to tears—but yet, *not quite*—and in consequence, not at all. His artistic seriousness is of an absolute nature, it is 'dead earnest playing'. But this intellectual seriousness is not absolute, it is only seriousness for the purposes of the game.
> 'Sufferings and Greatness of Richard Wagner'[1]

In *Felix Krull* the artist's interest in reality is purely a springboard for his creative work; in itself and for itself, reality is at odds with art's purpose. The need to create is the need to create illusions, and the artist's illusions are actually deceptions, a defeat rather than an exploration of reality.

Mann's irony here ruthlessly, though with a very light touch, reduces and distorts all theories of art as the expression of a higher truth, or as the integration of truths into a profound and concentrated whole. Eckermann reports Goethe as saying (April 10 1829) that the artist does not copy reality, but recomposes it to express truth; the pictures of Claude Lorraine, he says, have the highest truth, but no trace of actuality. The painter knew the real world by heart, down to the minutest details, but used it only to express the world of the soul; the truth evoked produces an illusion of actuality. Goethe's view underlies any belief that art has an importance other than entertainment, and that art's importance lies in the imagination's ability to reveal truths more profoundly and more vividly than could be revealed by straightforward report.

Mann does not ignore this view in *Felix Krull* nor does he deny that only such a view can explain the value and dignity one is inclined to grant to art's power; but his apparently genuine respect for such a theory of art actually undermines the value of those truths art is felt to express. When Krull feigns illness to avoid the tedium of school, he claims that his deception is based upon a higher truth—the truth that he is indeed unfit for school, because he finds it so tedious and because it cramps the education of the imagination, which is best developed by sleep. The same type of 'higher truth' lies behind his brilliant enactment of an epileptic fit during his army medical examination. Krull claims that only some outside power could have moulded his behaviour to such perfection—just as the artist frequently feels that his inspirations stems from an outside power. In the heat of creativeness the artist himself marvels at his work, and the artist's work in this novel is the work of the masquerader, the work of the playful deceiver; but the artist's respect for illusion is such that he, too, believes in the deceptions he creates; he, too, believes that they disclose a profound truth:

The comedy of this novel rests upon the refusal to distinguish between art as illusion and art as truth. Krull himself cannot recognise the validity of such a distinction—not because, as Goethe would have it, the higher truth evoked creates an illusion of actuality, but because successful illusion is the substance of art, and art's only criterion for truth. Art's purpose is to satisfy the imagination; the imagination is satisfied by illusion; when the imagination is satisfied it claims that its satisfaction is spiritual and that it has been satisfied by a vision of truth. Thus, the imagination, which dominates the characters in this novel, cannot distinguish between truth and illusion; truth is successful illusion. The success of this novel is remarkable, and reveals as incomplete any theory of art which does not take into account the amoral delight, the amoral appreciation of loveliness and perfection—in short, the purely imaginary impetus of art.

Felix Krull is a novel in the picaresque tradition, with a rogue, somewhat short of the criminal, as hero. He lives by his wits and his charm; he mingles with all social classes as he flits through life, and he writes his autobiography—the novel—in episodic fashion. The language of this novel achieves a polished, whimsical satire which has much the same point as the language of *The Magic Mountain*; here, too, delight signals danger, and decadence is bred in indolence, and indolence and dream seem far richer than practical, active life. The garish, terraced garden of Krull's childhood home, with its earthenware gnomes, aeolian harp and grottos, the cool subterranean wine cellars with their golden sap that will someday emerge from the twilight to evoke intoxication, irresponsibility and desire, the front door which emits the opening bars of Strauss's 'Freut euch des Lebens' as it closes—these are details which not only provide an artistic atmosphere alongside decadence, sensuality and indulgence, but which also point to a deception in the enterprise of the novel itself. The intricate detail—the 'truthfulness' of the work—is part of the fantasy. The attention to detail is a means of disguising the fictional aspect of the book, yet the wealth of detail reminds one that the purpose of the novel is to create illusion. What moral value or significance, Krull asks, can attach to confessions written from any point of view save that of truthfulness? So while this rogue pretends to be too honest to revert to the fables of the novelist, he underlines Mann's own roguishness as an artist; and just as Mann's 'faithful' recording of detail points to his job as a creator of illusion, Krull's attention to detail is the secret of his success as a masquerader and deceiver. Just as an artist is said to be 'truthful' when his imagination is at its best, Krull is most successful as an illusionist when he most careful and critically observes life.

After Krull's father dies and the family firm is liquidated (the family were wine producers and the firm's champagne had an elaborate label that was hardly commensurate, Krull admits, with the quality of the wine—thus his respect for appearance and indifference to substance is a family trait) he becomes something of a waif, but he finds his plight pitiful only because a youth as handsome as he should be forced to wear rags. In accordance with the picaresque tradition, this hero has some aspirations to a finer life; but Krull does not actually desire wealth—he desires to produce the illusion of wealth. His attention is naturally drawn to jewels, for jewels are symbols of wealth but worthless in themselves and capture people's hearts through loveliness alone. Indeed, an aesthete who wanted to plea for art's fundamental morality and concern for truth would have some difficulty accounting for the pleasure provided by jewels (or by the mere colour of paints or by sonority). Mann leaves no doubt as to the aesthetic richness of such pleasure. As cold creeps up Krull's poorly clad legs he stares into the windows of jewellry shops:

Pearl necklaces, palely shimmering on lace runners, arranged one
above the other, big as cherries in the middle and decreasing
symmetrically towards the sides, ending in diamond clasps, and
worth whole fortunes: diamond jewellry bedded on satin, sharply
glittering with all the colours of the rainbow and worthy to adorn
the neck, bosom, the head of queens; smooth golden cigarette cases
and cane heads, seductively displayed on glass shelves; and
everywhere, carelessly strewn, polished precious stones of mag-
nificent colour: blood-red rubies; grass-green, glossy emeralds;
transparent blue sapphires that held a star-shaped light; amethysts
whose precious violet shade is said to be due to organic content,
mother-of-pearl opals whose colour changed as I shifted my
position; single topazes; fanciful arrangements of gems in all the
shadings of the spectrum—all this was not only a joy to senses. I
studied it, I immersed myself completely in it, I tried to decipher
the few price-tags that were visible, I compared, I weighed by eye,
for the first time I became aware of my love for the precious stones
of the earth, those essentially worthless crystals whose elements
through a playful whim of nature have combined to form these
precious structures. It was at this time I laid the groundwork for my
later reliable connoisseurship in this magical domain.

Part 2, Chapter 4, p. 68[2]

The seriousness of Krull's study of the superficial, his notion of
profundity as a thorough observation of appearance, can be seen as a
parody of Nietzsche's respect for the Greeks' understanding of
nature's depth and for their courage in stopping at the surface to
admire appearance:

> Those Greeks were superficial—*out of profundity*. And is not this
> precisely what we are coming back to, we daredevils of the spirit
> who have climbed the highest and most dangerous peak of present
> thought and looked around from up there—we who have looked
> *down* from there? Are we not, precisely in this respect, Greeks?
> Adorers of forms, of tones, of words? and therefore—artists?[3]

Indeed, Krull's respect for appearance gives him, and stems from, a
sense of superiority. His ability to appreciate the superficial aspect of
life is part of his artistic detachment. He looks down upon life from
the height of his artistic—fraudulent purpose. He refuses to tear away
the veils of appearance, however, not because, like Nietzsche's

Greeks, he respects nature's depths, but because he prefers loveliness to the ugliness of reality and because he believes loveliness to be superior to reality. Krull's morality is an effete version of Nietzsche's master morality in which 'good' means that which is noble or beautiful, just as his belief that natural gifts such as talent and beauty indicate a man's true worth, is a version of Goethe's belief that natural gifts have a claim to moral esteem since they indicate God's favour. Krull reflects that most people believe nakedness to be levelling, that it is only dress which separates humankind into classes; he believes, on the contrary, that dress confuses the classes of humankind, and that nakedness reveals people in their true order of merit—nakedness reveals people's true appearance, and upon that is based their true merit. Mann, through Krull's devotion to appearance, mocks esteem for beauty. He shows the love of appearances to issue from a recalcitrant shallowness, but at the same time he shows appearances to satisfy all spiritual craving. The comedy of *Felix Krull* exposes the fact that people do not need truth, and that they feel the need for no values other than those represented by the masquerader.

The hero of a picaresque novel flouts society's rules by wandering easily from class to class, and in his wanderings he both observes and partakes in social comedy. Here people's vanity, greed and sexual desire spring up through elegant and expensive surfaces with a predictability that actually enhances rather than undermines the comedy. The language of the novel is marvellously suited to the casual, disdainful, adept observation of manners. Among the guests in Krull's childhood home is a 'Jewish banker with a wife who awesomely overflowed her jet-embroidered dress in every direction';[4] and when the family goes on holiday Krull's 'father was taking mud-baths for his gout, and [his] mother and sister made themselves conspicuous on the promenade with the exaggerated size of their hats'.[5] The characters' language, too, makes them subjects of a comedy of manners. The Marquis de Venosta, in describing his argument with his parents, tells Krull, 'I assured them in a voice that was both deep and vibrant, that I was sincerely sorry to be a source of concern for them',[6] and Venosta's mother writes to her son expressing worry over his soul—that is, she explains, she worries about his social salvation. The focus of the comedy, however, is not social criticism; it is the play of illusion against reality and the power of beauty and the universal desire to be enchanted by illusion, to be deluded to the point at which reality disappears.

Krull's first exploit as a masquerader is as a performer in an orchestra with a violin bow so heavily greased that, as he moves it across the strings, it makes no sound. Yet his gestures are so feverish and hectic, and his expression so intense, that the audience is enchanted. The image of the performer, not the sound he actually produces, provides the greatest satisfaction. The emptiness of the appearance in no way detracts from its value, for it is only the superficial which people crave. The play of appearance is necessary because 'real life' is unbearable; yet in *Felix Krull* life is unbearable not in Nietzschean terms of inexorable pain and power, but through emptiness and boredom. This is the justification of art, and thus the need for art, which is itself mere play, arises from a life which is itself empty. Krull's godfather enjoys dressing up the boy in various costumes to serve as a model for his painting. Krull adores these exotic clothes, which inspire his adaptable personality to assume the character of the costume's period and country. In returning to his ordinary outfit and therefore to the ordinary world, he suffers what he claims to be an indescribable boredom. Only a greater enchantment—only the pleasures of sex—can console him for the loss of the imaginary world. And in this shallow world, naturally, sex, which Krull calls 'The Great Joy', is allied to the redeeming, frivolous world of the imagination; it is sensual ecstasy combined with a deceptive sense of the spiritual. The only value in this world arises from the masquerade. When the masquerade is superseded by reality, sensual pleasure is the only compensation. Krull must be careful to preserve the enchantments which the world allows him. He must refrain from sensual indulgence lest sensual pleasure and the delight of illusion grow pale. He must reject the proposals of a young heiress and a Scottish lord, not only to avoid the tedium of starting a family or becoming enmeshed in a homosexual affair, but to avoid being tied to reality. Krull is an artist and therefore he does not want an actual, prosaic realisation of his ambitions for wealth and glamour. The pleasures of illusion are insubstantial and can easily disappear, but they are the only pleasures in life, and therefore they must be carefully preserved.

Mann's peculiarly limiting view of art as something which pleases not through profundity or truth but through shallowness and deception is part of this novel's comedy. Nonetheless, the success of the comedy rests upon its success as a serious investigation of the nature of art's effect and the nature of art as a human need. Mann, however, refuses to distinguish between the immediate, sensuous aspect of aesthetic response and the undeniable aesthetic satisfaction of artistic truth which is not a clever semblance of the actual but a critical investigation of the actual. This refusal seems plausible partly because Mann fails to distinguish in this novel between the creative and the performing artist. The latter can, of course, be creative, but his stock-in-trade is immediate effect and appearance in a way the composer's or writer's is not. In this novel Mann's interest is primarily in the performing artist. As a result, the burden of longing Hanno Buddenbrook suffered, the burden of an unexpressed imagination and of life's constraint, becomes, in Felix Krull (at his first visit to the theatre) an enchantment liberated by comedy, and an enchantment spun by illusion, unencumbered by the groping expressiveness of the creative artist:

> But how can one describe the fever of excitement that possessed me when we drove in a cab to the theatre and entered the auditorium with its tiers of boxes? The women fanning their bosoms in the balconies, the men leaning over their chairs to chat; the hum and buzz of conversation in the orchestra, where we presently took our seats; the odours which streamed from hair and clothing to mingle with that of the illuminating-gas; the confusion of sounds as the orchestra tuned up; the voluptuous frescoes that depicted whole cascades of rosy, foreshortened nymphs—certainly all this could not but rouse my youthful sense and prepare my mind for the extraordinary scene to come. Never before except in Church had I seen people gathered together in a large and stately auditorium [. . .] certainly all this was in my eyes a temple of pleasure, where men in need of edification gathered in darkness and gazed upward open-mouthed into a realm of brightness and perfection where they beheld their heart's desire.
>
> Part 1, chapter 5, pp. 22–3

The references to religion and edification and perfection and fulfilment, alongside the obvious vanity and frivolity, both propose and then immediately deny the theory that art is a source of learning and spiritual revelation. Here Mann does not warn, as he does in *The Magic Mountain*, against the fascination which seems to be heavenly but which is actually dæmonic; here he does not try to expose the magic that confuses values; for here illusion is the highest value, the only value, and it is only through illusion that the audience will behold their heart's desire.

The star of the operetta that introduces the fourteen-year-old Krull to the theatrical world is Müller-Rosé. This man is dazzling bright even though he is dressed in black. His clothes are so well pressed that they could not last a quarter of an hour in real life. On stage this man is a transhuman being, but in his dressing room, Krull discovers, he is grotesque. Off-stage his painted face looks ridiculous. He exudes a stink of sweat and grease. Horrible red-rimmed suppurating pustules cover the actor's back and arms. Yet he has not cheated the audience by appearing so beautifully before them. The audience did not want to observe the real person as they gazed upwards, openmouthed, towards the bright stage. They wanted to behold their heart's desire—which is the illusion of God-implanted perfection. On stage the artist, through skilled practice of musical and dramatic conventions, is a higher being. Freed from ordinary life, he dispenses what Krull wants to call 'the joy of life—if that phrase can be used to describe the precious and painful feeling, compounded of envy, yearning, hope and love, that the sight of beauty and light-hearted perfection kindles in the hearts of men'.[7] Krull's praise of the actor's function reads like Nietzsche's justification of a morality based upon the noble and the beautiful. The audience are grateful for their subjection; they are grateful for this superior manifestation. Their subjection is compounded, however, by the fact that they know this manifestation is an illusion. Their smiles are both silly and blissful, for they know their delight depends upon deception. The artist is an entertainer, and the purpose of his work is to please; in deceiving his audience, he gives them the vision they desire.

The other artist who fascinates Krull and who teaches him about the artist's necessary isolation from the world is a trapeze performer who refuses to use a safety net. Her skill depends upon such fine calculation, Krull muses, that she could not possibly tolerate the distractions of ordinary human affections and attachments. The skill which keeps her airborne is inhuman: it is, in a sense, purely physical, and in that respect it is animal; but it is also finely calculated and demands supreme concentration, and in that respect she is transhuman. Such a being has no involvement in the common world; the ground below her, the world of humanity, into which she would fall if her art failed her, is the death of the artist.

These are performing artists, resembling Krull in their achievement of illusion, but the language used to describe their purposes and effects classes them with creative artists. Müller-Rosé's audience is like 'an enormous swarm of nocturnal insects, silently, blindly, and blissfully rushing into the blazing fire'.[8] Müller-Rosé is the hypnotic flame which attracts and destroys, just as, in Charlotte Kestner's eyes,

Goethe is the flame which sacrifices everything to his art. The liberation from the common world of humanity is the destructive liberation against which Charlotte struggles; it is an entry into the world of irresponsibility and wildness and endless possibility. Nevertheless, the features upon which Mann focuses and which lead Krull to the conclusion that the artist is a subhuman and transhuman being (part animal, part angel) are peculiar to the performing artist. It is the skill of the performing, not the creative, artist that demands such perfect timing as the trapeze woman exhibits, skill which denies human fallibility and the personal self. It is the performing, not the creative artist who offers elegance so perfect that it could not last a quarter of an hour in real life. Moreover, the need to please an audience is different in the different types of artist. In *Felix Krull* 'powerful' art means 'art which entertains and enchants'. A powerful performer makes an immediate impact on his audience; in a given period of time, he must captivate them and delight them. The creative artist's need to please, however, is no more than his need to communicate and to reveal his vision. The power of art comes from the sense that the artist has got something right—and this sense of rightness is related to a sense of truth and depth. Powerful art at least seems to be profound, and to reveal or to touch upon something in reality. *Felix Krull* denies not only the profundity, but the impression of profundity or truth. Such a denial is discerning comedy only if the performing artist is taken as a model of the artist *per se*, for the performing artist must concentrate upon illusion and effect and measure truth by art to an extent that makes Mann's exaggeration plausible.

This assumption that the needs of the imagination are superficial resolves the tension expressed in Mann's other works between imagination and life. Felix Krull does not suffer Hanno's paralytic impasse or Tonio Kröger's alienation because, as a performing artist, whose life is his performance, he does not suffer the constraints of the actual and the commonplace. As an artist whose life is one with his art, he understands his purpose as lifting reality into the world of the imagination. In *The Magic Mountain* and *Death in Venice* Mann's Romanticist view of the imagination was of a force that combined the dangerous, the dreadful and the alluring, but Felix Krull is undaunted by dark abysses and chaotic urges. His superficiality is his assurance and his salvation. He has a sanity Hans Castorp, Aschenbach, and Hanno lack, because he quite happily accepts life as it is—yet he accepts it because, for him, life is simply material for his art.

The Romantic tension between imagination and life is resolved because imagination is sufficient unto itself. Felix Krull is not burdened by a death wish—first, because his imagination is attracted only by the elegant and the fair (unlike Hans Castorp's fascination for disease and Aschenbach's susceptibility to primitive impulses) and, secondly, because his imagination is satisfied by illusion, and does not crave expression or integration with the deeper sources of life.

Imagination involves reverence for elegance and beauty, and elegance and beauty are concerned with form and appearance alone; they are indifferent to moral content. When, as a child, Krull steals sweets from a shop, he denies that his action is a case of common theft. The sensual delight of his wares and the magical ease of his act provide entry to that art world, that dream world in which ordinary laws and prosaic restrictions are suspended. The word 'theft', Krull admits, in some sense applies; but more important, more real, is the unique deed 'forever shining with newness and originality'. Keats said that the imagination derives as much pleasure from creating an Iago as an Imogen; and it is this type of artistic indifference to moral content which Mann comically exploits in the theft episode and distorts to make a point about the immorality of the aesthetic consciousness. For the pleasure of creating an Iago is the pleasure of revealing evil—the pleasure of revealing one aspect of human reality. The artist can exult in the vividness and power of his creation; he can (as Verdi does in his Iago) share the character's exultation in evil; but the portrayal of evil as clearly evil shows a distinct moral concern. The theft scene in *Felix Krull* presents an argument for imagination's indifference to morality because imagination is concerned only with grace and elegant trickery and beauty. It cannot reveal either evil or goodness; its substance is only the play of appearance. Yet imagination dominates life because life itself has nothing of greater value to offer mankind. What makes this novel more than a critique of aestheticism, what pushes the comedy over the brink of nihilism, is the fact that the dissociation of imagination and truth is a result not only of the superficiality of the imagination but the superficiality of life itself.

There is no depth in life, and the imagination does not need to grapple with profound and dæmonic sources to survive. Like all Mann's artists, Krull is attached to some kind of underworld (through sleep, for which he says he has always had a remarkable talent); but Krull's underworld is not unending strife or passion or unreflecting, dæmonic energy. Krull's underworld of sleep and dream and of the spacious wine cellars he explored as a child, is indolence and indulgence. Sleep provides him with the power to absorb the world's sights accurately. The most important understanding, Krull believes, is gained not by exertion but by breathing in the secret machinery of the universe. Such methods of learning presuppose a calmly run universe, and Krull's talent for sleep is disturbed when Professor Kuckuck discusses the vast expanse of the universe, the transitory nature of Being, the ambiguous division between the organic and inorganic, the continual joy and labour of Being. Professor Kuckuck's Schopenhauerian vision of an active universe strains Krull's imagination. His insomniac excitement can be read as a parody of Thomas Buddenbrook's metaphysical ecstasy.

Krull is an artist of image and dream, not of the forceful, primal will. His usually perfect composure is upset by this new awareness of the vastness and energy of Being. His excitement is akin to 'The Great Joy' of sex; and the volume closes (though Mann had planned to write a sequel) with Krull's embrace of a female representative (the professor's wife) of this primordial force. But in this novel even the Dionysian force is part of the comedy and in keeping with the novel's message of life's frivolity. The bullfight in which the Dionysian urge emerges might have been a trite Freudian allegory, were it not for the irresistable combination of assurance and absurdity that runs throughout the novel. Into the ring runs a steer:

> black, heavy, mighty, a visibly irresistible concentration of procreative, murderous force, in which earlier, older people certainly saw a god-animal, the animal god, with little threatening horns affixed to his broad forehead, bending a little upward at the points and clearly charged with death.
>
> Part 3, chapter 11, p. 337

This elemental, sexual-aggressive force quickly reveals its comic aspect as the proud Iberian woman proclaims her love for Krull: 'a whirlwind of primordial forces seized me and bore me into the realm of ecstasy. And high and stormy, under my ardent caresses, stormier than at the Iberian game of blood, I saw the surging of that queenly bosom'.[9] Just as the beautiful has been relegated to charm and illusion, the deepest life energies are presented as a 'game of blood' and issue in a hilarious rather than a dreadful or awesome passion.

Krull is a perfect embodiment of the Apollonian image. He himself represents an Apollonian vision; he is extremely handsome, with meltingly blue eyes, tawny skin, blond hair and a wonderfully proportioned physique. He is also himself an Apollonian artist, for his inspiration is the world of dream and his purpose is to create beautiful, ethereal visions in compensation for the drabness of life. Yet even as Krull appears to speak for Nietzsche's assessment of art, he mocks the philosopher's theories. Nietzsche saw Apollonian art—the art of beauty, proportion, grace—as arising from a recognition of the inexorable pain of existence, as compensation for the life which defies man's spiritual needs. Krull, too, claims that beauty is man's salvation from a wretched life and that beauty is necessary to the spirit; but his claim is comic, for the novel shows beauty clearly to be indulgence and delusion. Beauty is not the spirit's realisation; it is abnegation of spirit. When the intellectual novelist Dianne Philibert invites Krull to make love to her, she explains that the intellect longs for the delights of the non-intellect. The intellect longs, she tells him, to kneel before the stupidity of beauty in an ecstasy of self-abnegation and self-degradation. She is not in love with Krull, not with him personally, but with him as the image of youthful beauty. Krull's beauty, and the love he inspires, is like Tadzio's beauty and, like Dianne Philibert, Aschenbach (also an intellectual novelist) loves the boy for what he represents, and the drama of his passion is a drama of his intellect's abnegation and degradation. Yet in *Felix Krull* Aschenbach's story is released from its tragic impasse. Krull's episode with the novelist is a triumph of comedy. The intoxication of degradation is part of the warm, human absurdity of sexual attraction. The intoxication has an exuberance that prevents the degradation from being actually destructive. The characters accept themselves as comic beings and are saved from Aschenbach's desperation. Nevertheless, even in face of this comic liberation, the soul is shown to be defeated. The soul, or the needs of the spirit, cannot be expressed in terms of human impulses and desires. The power and satisfactions of beauty are delightfully portrayed; but beauty provides fulfilment because it ignores the spirit, and just as *Felix Krull* presents beauty's delights, it denies their value.

Emotions and intellect and spirit are defenceless against beauty: the book asserts that master morality is fact. One of the most striking episodes in the novel is Zouzou's battle against her attraction to Krull—that is, to beauty and grace and illusion. Her resistance and her uncertainty of his seriousness are similar to Imma Spoelman's inability to trust and inability to gauge the sincerity of Prince Heinrich's wooing; but while Mann, in *Royal Highness*, treats the problem of the relation between an attractive image and inner worth and reality as a genuine problem, in *Felix Krull* the problem is only a confusion. In *Royal Highness* image is shown to need the sustenance of spirit, but in *Felix Krull* (the first part of which was written at about the same time as *Royal Highness*) image supplies all human needs, and it is mere prejudice—and a destructive prejudice—to demand more than beauty for one's substantial needs. Zouzou quotes Krull a hymn about stench and corruption of the inner soul which abide in spite of a fair outward appearance. To Krull the sentiments expressed in the hymn are blasphemous, because they deny the reality and supremacy of beauty. What would become of life, he demands, if there were no longer belief in image and dream, in appearance and the surface of things? His sermon reads very much like Nietzsche's injunction to the men of the future to be too gay, too experienced, too profound to disturb all the veils of appearance; but Nietzsche's advocacy of the superficial is based upon the assumption that in being lighthearted and apparently shallow one is acknowledging and respecting life's depths. Krull's respect for the superficial, however, is based upon the belief that the superficial itself is of the utmost significance, that imagination as illusion is the highest and most profound reality.

Felix Krull abandons the Romanticist's image of imagination straining towards the unattainable. Imagination's purpose is to construct a world more real, more valuable than life, but there is here no tragic opposition between imagination and life, for life's claims are shown to be innocuous and people do not need to find fulfilment within the actual world. Krull is on very good terms with reality; he values it because it offers material to his imagination. With Don Quixote's ingenuousness, Krull sees the world as a vast and infinitely enticing phenomenon, offering him priceless satisfactions and fully worthy of his attention and solicitude. Krull transforms the drab life of the Buddenbrooks, which was seen to be unworthy of practical effort; but unlike Don Quixote, Krull does not see an idealised life. He sees life as it is, and studies it, interested in the actuality for the use he can make of it in his deceptions.

Krull is an artist, and therefore he must maintain his distance from life. A close personal attachment, he feels, will sap his energy and concentration; the physical pleasures of sex enervate him by satisfying him too completely. The separation between art and life is not forced upon him by a gigantic, mystical longing; rather, the separation is carefully chosen and carefully preserved. Life, taken merely as appearance and as material for imaginative visions, is thoroughly satisfying, and Krull, as an artist, must guard against its satisfactions, for yearning is the artist's inspiration. Art is no longer the curse the melancholic Tonio Kröger feels it to be; art is no longer life's negation and defeat. In *Felix Krull* art is the supreme fulfilment, and imagination supplies one's deepest needs. Art fulfils because the demands of morality and of the spirit are shown to be unreal. Therefore, the nihilism of this novel rests upon its resolution between art and life, a resolution achieved by the recognition that human needs are satisfied by illusion and deception. Yet the vitality of the novel camouflages its own message. There is a liberation from the plodding self-distrust that weighs upon *The Magic Mountain*, but the refreshment and charm of the comedy disguise its exposure of the essence of the human spirit as frivolity.

9 Dæmonic Redemption

In Mann's early works artistic sensibility was presented as an impasse. Hanno Buddenbrook's burden of longing isolated him from life, and his alienation could be resolved only by death. The poet in *Royal Highness* says that his literary talent is a sign of his life-inadequacy. Aschenbach's detachment, which is necessary to his work, leads to the bewilderment that destroys him. The power of art and of the artist's creativeness crush these characters. Either the unwieldly forces of artistic sensibility are channelled into art (and are thereby channelled off from life) or they become wild and destructive. After *Death in Venice* Mann's interests gradually turned to the problem of artistic power as success rather than impasse. What would happen if someone were strong enough to survive the upsurge of these forces and to make use of them? What, in short, would be the result if the artist excercised his creative powers upon life?

Felix Krull is such an artist. His effect was to bring pleasure into the world, but the pleasure depended upon an ultimate nihilism; it satisfies because mankind, in the world of this novel, does not need reality or morality. The nihilism upon which Krull thrives is both comic and charming, because Krull is an Apollonian artist; his subject is dream, elegance, proportion, illusion. In *Mario and the Magician* and *Doctor Faustus* Krull's comedy turns to horror, for the life-artists here are artists of the Will; they discover and celebrate the most primitive and urgent and intractable impulses.

During the First World War Mann had declared the artist to be a non-political man. His works, therefore, should not be given a political interpretation, for politics, Mann said, was a separate field that should be left to the experts. *The Magic Mountain*, published nine years after his plea for the artist's political innocence — *Meditations of a Non-Political Man*, 1915—shows a distinct fear of imagination's influences upon political life; and in the thirties, with the growth of Fascism in Europe and, in particular, of Nazism in Germany, Mann came to see distorted political practices as another face of artistic powers. German Romanticism—its sympathy with death and the dæmonic, its appeal to the popular folk element, its regard for instinct, its refusal to compromise emotional intensity—was particularly susceptible to political misuse. Indeed, any political use of Romanticism would, Mann supposed, be disastrous, for in the political sphere Romanticism became a celebration and exploitation of instinct, a spurning of a humanist morality on the grounds that any denial or restraint of instinct is pure hypocrisy. The Romantic folk element became a national fairytale that led to an archaic blood brotherhood, which encouraged destruction of everything outside the narrow collective.

Mann often spoke of Wagner as a magician or wizard, and he signed his own letters to his family 'Z' for '*Zauberer*' (magician). The artist is a magician because he explores the dangerous depths of the psyche and has the power to present anything at all in a desirable light. The artist's personal unconscious speaks with a collective voice, and this collective voice can rouse the collective will, which is an amoral and violent will. The political despot has this same magical power, this magical power of discovering and manipulating people's urges and desires. Albert Speer says of one such despot:

> . . . Hitler no longer seemed to be speaking to convince; rather, he seemed to feel that he was expressing what the audience, by now transformed into a single mass, expected of him . . .
>
> Both Goebbels and Hitler had understood how to unleash mass instincts at their meetings, how to play on the passions that underlay the veneer of ordinary respectable life . . . But as I see it today, these politicians in particular were in fact moulded by the mob itself, guided by its yearnings and its daydreams.[1]

Mario and the Magician, written in 1933, presents precisely this kind of despot. The magician is a hybrid of the artist and politician. His purpose as mass hypnotiser is not camouflaged by the aura of a political campaign nor is his mass vision decorated by artistic taste. He represents, starkly, in its nastiest aspect, the malevolent power of the artist's sensibility.

The drama of *Mario and the Magician*, like that of *Death in Venice*, is embedded within the atmospheric setting. In many respects the atmosphere is similar to that of the earlier novella for the tale takes place in an Italian seaside resort with a heat that breeds both indolence and wildness; but whereas the debilitation and corruption of Venice mark a spiritual or imaginative striving that has failed, Torre di

Venere wallows in the vulgar and the banal. Illbred merrymakers, with full-throated, hideously stressed cries, crowd the beach and cafés. The German family is not seduced by beauty but by the coarse and the commonplace. Inert and fascinated, they remain at the resort despite the cheap upsurge of national fervour which expresses itself as hostility towards foreigners. The German family believe that in staying they are facing up to life's difficulties, that they are exhibiting admirable resolution, but this moral stance is only a subterfuge for their attraction to the sinister atmosphere.

The sinister is magnetic, but it has none of the lush sense of promise that dwelt within Aschenbach's degrading visions. However repulsive the object, the magician can make it desirable: this is the point and horror of the tale. Freedom does not lie in the ability to carry out the impulses of the will, for the will is subject to the crudest influences and delusions. The magician Cipolla persuades his audience to act according to their will, and he proves that such 'freedom' disgusts them. Sipping cognac, smoking the cheapest brand of cigarettes and exhaling the smoke through his rotting teeth, looking like a circus director with his foppish air and black-varnished, frizzled hair, he preys upon people's hidden desires and frustrations, and uses this sympathy to manipulate them. The audience pities the youth upon whom Cipolla first excercises his power, for the youth appears to be in convulsions of pain; but Cipolla tells his audience that he himself is the one in pain, and that the youth is simply expressing what the magician actually feels. Cipolla so keenly sympathises with those people over whom he exercises his power that he himself is burdened by their feelings. His power, though obviously malevolent, has an aspect of loving patronage; his manipulation is a sympathetic participation in the people's will.

Cipolla's audience is slow to understand that the magician's stunts are more than a game, that they are truly his subjects, and that their wills can be so easily touched by the will of another. Innocence is no protection against such influences. The children of the German couple find Cipolla's stunts inexpressibly delightful; innocence applauds this evil, finding it a marvellous entertainment. Cipolla, as artist-tyrant, can captivate the pious and ethereal Signora Angioliere. She would follow him to the ends of the earth, while her husband's voice, the voice of love and duty, remains unheard. She beholds in the vulgar, deformed magician the realisation of her highest dreams, just as the audience in *Felix Krull* saw in Müller-Rosé their heart's desire; but the magician works directly upon the will; he does not captivate by beauty or by any other means that contain something of value. He is pure power, and purely revolting. Cipolla convinces the waiter Mario—the man whose duty is to serve and who therefore serves the magician's will—that he, the foul-breathed old man, is the infinitely desirable Sylvestra, and Mario passionately kisses the magician. Realising his mistake, realising that his senses can be totally at odds with his soul's desire, Mario shoots the magician. The narrator admits that he is relieved to see the magician dead, for he has witnessed the horrific effect of a man who persuades the people to act according to their will.

The will cannot be taught to discriminate either beauty from ugliness or good from evil: that is the pessimistic message of this tale. The tension between life and imagination is no longer the dominant theme; the problem is life's use of imagination. In Hanno's musical sensibility he discovered the burden of endless striving, but the practical world thwarted the yearning and only in death could he find release. When imagination has a practical direction, however, the death impulse becomes a destructive impulse. The man who can survive Aschenbach's trial, the man who has the artist's knowledge of the abyss as well as practical ability, is the magician-tyrant.

Mann's conception of art and its dangers, his fascination with death and the dæmonic, his distrust of his own enthusiasms, are all concentrated in his attitude towards music. This attitude was formed by the opposing influences of Nietzsche and Wagner. From Nietzsche he learned to be critical of Romanticism and to try to master that 'seductive master complex of the soul, the musical-Romantic and Romantic-musical—and thus almost the German—complex'[2] for the sake of life and the future. All that he learned of good and of triumph over Romantic seductions, he felt he owed to Nietzsche; all that he knew of evil's temptation and the longing to relinquish life and purpose, he owed to Wagner.[3]

With the rise of Nazism he came to see the problem of German Romanticism as *the* German problem. Nazism was an extension and distortion of the German-Romantic soul which had become cruel and barbaric under the influence of magician-leader. *Doctor Faustus* is a novel about this German impasse. It traces the conservative, pious folk elements of old Germany, in which the Germanic race was simple and wholesome and its nationalism was pride in German characteristics rather than hostility towards and ignorance of other national cultures, to the national travesty of Nazism in which barbarism passes for realism and honesty, and the peculiarly German-Romantic sympathy with impulse and death becomes a celebration of violence. The creative myths of old Germany become political pragmatism, and a political nightmare.

Aesthetics and psychology turned into politics: that is the substance of Mann's analysis of Nazism. What is an honest, worthy struggle for the artist or psychologist—a struggle with the hidden and often chaotic psychic energies for which he seeks creative or intellectual realisation—opens, in the political sphere, the door to every conceivable cruelty. The novel does not deal with the specific tenets of National Socialism, nor does it expose in detail the atrocities of the Third Reich, nor does it place much emphasis upon the responsibility of an individual's behaviour. The narrator Zietblom is a commonplace, ineffectual German who would never actually condone the government's cruelties but who does not take any steps to discover the true nature of his government. He would pass for a reasonable man, and towards the end of the war he actually hopes that his country will be defeated; yet, initially, he was proud of Germany's swift victories, and his criticism of the government is couched in modest terms: 'I have never,' he admits, 'precisely in regard to the Jewish problem, been able fully to agree with our Führer and his paladins'. [4] Clearly, Mann is critical of such innocuous protest, but this criticism is a minor point. He focuses upon the general philosophical atmosphere of prewar Germany and blames the malevolent licence of thought—rather than inflation and unemployment—for Germany's national aggrandisement and moral decline. His view of Nazism as a result of Romanticism's proneness to corruption limits the political and historical interest of his study, but this novel is, nonetheless, a tremendous success. The intricate interweaving of themes does not supply merely an intellectual diagram (as it frequently does in *The Magic Mountain*) but presents a moral drama, and the drama has a thoroughly convincing necessity.

Doctor Faustus is subtitled 'The life of the German composer Adrian Leverkühn as told by a friend'. The focus of the novel is on music—German music—and the course of Leverkühn's creative, artistic history is interwoven with and sometimes parallel to the political history of Germany. Leverkühn himself is not involved in the political world but, through his unconscious sympathy with the spirit of his age (through his artistic sensibility) he himself enacts, in his creative life, the tumultuous atmosphere and moral confusion which erupts under Hitler's government. The composer's dissatisfaction with classical forms, his sense that they are unsuited to the expression of the modern soul and that they can no longer be used seriously, but only in parody, mirrors his contemporaries' awareness of their outworn morality. Modern consciousness has become too sophisticated to accept the moral precepts of bourgeois humanism or the shallow view of man as a rational being upon which such moral precepts rest. The Kridwiss circle can only parody the old moral assumptions. They see themselves as exhibiting a characteristically German honesty in facing the multi-dimensional aspects of man; they dismiss as hypocrisy the morality that assumes human nature to be capable of attaining reliability and altruism. If one no longer treats the old humanist morality as an irrefutable premise, they argue, then logic does not compel one to reinstate it. In this circle, the German penchant for tragedy becomes a penchant for sadism, and the prospect of chaos—which will result from the moral revolution advocated in this circle—is welcomed. The old morality must be destroyed, and the ensuing violence is seen as a fine test of the German character.

Alongside Germany's need to establish a national self-definition and alongside society's need to discover a morality that could take into account the modern view of man as a largely irrational and amoral being, is Adrian Leverkühn's need to establish new principles of musical composition. These new principles must satisfy the intellectual demands of music and provide the possibility of objective organisation, an organisation that is necessary to music as communication. At the same time, these forms must allow emotive—sensuous—spiritual expression; they must supply an objective organisation of personal expression, as does a language. The problem is too drastic to be solved simply by developing another musical form—something just a little different from the sonata or rondo. The problem can be solved only by a new conception of form. For essential to classical form is the appearance of ease and fluidity and grace. Classical forms attempt to solve the problem of structure and expression as though the problem never existed. With great care the classical composer presented a work which seemed effortless. Musical forms were thought to be God-given forms, reflecting the logic and harmony of the universe, and the composer used these forms to express a soul that delighted in universal laws. Contemporary man, having no belief in a universe whose ultimate reality can be expressed in elegance, ease and harmony, can only mock classical forms. Mockery, however, is limited; it is purely negative, and the contemporary composer seeks a positive language for the modern upheaval and violence. The Germans accepted a highly regimented government to provide form for the contemporary glorification of instinct; the National Socialists offered discipline in a time of chaos, and the impression of energy in an atmosphere of hopelessness. In parallel, Leverkühn develops a rigorous method of composition in which no note is free; that is, every note is derived from the original, chosen series, the notes of which always appear in the same order, though they can be ordered vertically and well as horizontally and can be varied through inversion, retrograde inversion and crab-figures imitation. This compositional method provides a musical form which—unlike classical forms—is indifferent to harmony and melody. Leverkühn's arbitrarily chosen series undercuts the assumption of an ultimately rational God-given basis for musical form and escapes the pleasing conventions of classical styles.

Adrian Leverkühn's compositional method is of course derived from Schoenberg's serial compositions. While Mann was writing *Doctor Faustus* he and Schoenberg were neighbours in California—both were exiles from Hitler's Germany. Mann had the opportunity to see some of the composer's scores, and Leverkühn's penultimate oratorio, *Apocalypsis cun figuris*, is similar to Schoenberg's *Jakobsleiter*, though this work had not yet been performed. Schoenberg's subsequent quarrel with Mann over this novel involved, more than Mann's presumption that the serial composer had sold his soul to the devil, Mann's attribution of serial composition to a chracter without explaining that the method was really Schoenberg's. The musician's hostility towards the novelist for the theft was compounded by Schoenberg's belief that what the novelist had stole he had not got right; Schoenberg denied that his method was as rigorously determined as Mann made Leverkühn's out to be. Schoenberg was partly to blame for Mann's misinterpretation; for the composer himself overemphasised the importance of the series as a unifying principle of his works (which are in fact unified by texture and expression and mood at least as much as by the series) and he did not advertise the fact that he frequently deviated from the series when the series did not provide the sound he wanted. Mann was influenced by Theodor Adorno's *Philosophy of Modern Music* in his assessment of the impersonal rigour of serial composition; but though *Doctor Faustus* reveals Mann's misgivings as to the creative flexibility of twelve-tone composition, this method does provide a form for Leverkühn's message; he achieves the artistic breakthrough which supplies a moral-psychological musical expression of the modern soul.

Schopenhauer saw music as a direct expression of the Will, and Mann shared the view that music, of all the arts, had the closest affinity to the seething, preintellectual forces that lie behind life and death. Kierkegaard, too, saw music as primarily an expression of the dæmonic: immediate sensuousness was music's proper subject, and all other uses of music were secondary or derivative. Mann, however, was sensitive to music's ability to combine the utmost sensuousness with the most sublime spirituality, so that if music actually was the devil's language it nonetheless seemed to be God's language. Moreover, he was (unlike Schopenhauer and Kierkegaard) greatly interested in the intellectual aspect of music and in the way this seemed to be at odds with the licence and yearning of music's content. Kretzschmar, Leverkühn's teacher, says that music is a Kundry who wills not what she does: music is primarily intellectual, and its sumptuous sounds defy its essentially intellectual purpose. Music's intellectual purpose is refined spiritual expression, but music's spirituality is always ambiguous, and can be sustained only by overcoming its other sensuous and dæmonic enchantments.

With its double danger of the barbaric will and sensuousness, music presents the Romanticist's most compelling temptations, and only a hero can survive it. Mann saw Nietzsche's struggle in this light. Music, he said, tried the heroic nature of Nietzsche's soul, and through this temptation he found resolution and redemption.[5] Adrian Leverkühn is in many respects modelled on Nietzsche. Some of the incidents in his character's life are drawn directly from Deussen's memoirs of the philosopher. Nietzsche and Leverkühn each tried to escape his emotional isolation by making a proposal of marriage to a highly intelligent, attractive and popular young woman (Nietzsche's woman was Lou Andréas-Salomé, and Leverkühn's was the set designer Marie Godeau), yet each ruined his chances by sending a messenger (Nietzsche sent Paul Rée) who became himself the successful suitor. Leverkühn's trip to the Liepzig brothel, where, unaware, he is led by an anonymous guide, is based upon Nietzsche's experience. The philosopher walked directly to the piano, struck a few chords (chords which echo the Hermit's prayer in *Der Freischütz*), and left the brothel, but, a year later, by some frightful compulsion, he returned to the brothel and contracted syphilis. Both the fictional composer and the philosopher saw the disease as a means of heightening their creative powers; both, therefore, sacrificed their health and the possibility of a love attachment on the basis of a very cruel assessment of the demands of their work. The composer, like the philosopher, is disdainful of a safe, comfortable morality and both, though themselves physically weak, exult in man's dæmonic strengths and urges. Just as Nietzsche (or, rather Nietzsche edited by his anti-Semitic sister) was used in the political sphere to justify mass cruelty, Leverkühn's denial (through a rejection of classical forms) of the harmony between man's soul and the divine, and his alignment of the modern soul with the devil, is reflected, in the political world, as the abnegation of morality. The results of Nietzsche's work were disastrous; the political reflection of Leverkühn's consciousness is disastrous; yet in both cases Mann saw a hero and, ultimately, a triumphant hero—a Romantic saviour who depicts hope through devastation and despair.

Mann's love for Nietzsche obviously influenced his portrayal of the composer, for, despite Leverkühn's aloofness, the character has a thoroughly convincing magnetism and commands total sympathy. Leverkühn's laughter, his mocking manner and his blue-black eyes continually remind one of his isolating purposefulness and dæmonic intensity; yet this cold vividness presents an extremely appealing character. As a child, when Adrian's father shows him how nature uses deception and illusion as a means for survival (as in camouflage and in mimicry of dangerous animals) his laugh is a slight expulsion of air from the nose and mouth, with

> a toss of the head at the same time, short cool, yes contemptuous, or at the most as though he would say: 'Good, that; droll, curious amusing!' But his eyes were taking it in; their gaze was distant and strange, and their darkness, metal-sprinkled, had taken on a deeper shade.
>
> Chapter 4, p. 33

Similarly, when Zeitblom complains that Adrian, in his series of songs taken from the *Purgatorio* and the *Paradiso*, has set only the cruellest passages in Dante to music, Leverkühn responds:

> Mute, veiled, musing, aloof to the point of offensiveness, full of a chilling melancholy [his glance] ended in a smile with closed lips, not unfriendly, yet mocking, and with that gesture of turning away, so long familiar to me.
>
> Chapter 20, p. 158

The laughter, Zeitblom says, is clearly not an expression of humour, but a desire to escape his stern consciousness. Laughter also plays an important part in Adrian's music; it is excitement and mockery in the face of suffering; it is the devil's response to the confusing amalgamation of good and evil and damnation and salvation, which, over and over again, is a theme of Adrian's music, as it was a theme of his professors' theology. In this way Mann uses a personal characteristic to reveal a psychological and moral difficulty. The frequency with which such a description is repeated, and the number of its associations, give it the character of a *leitmotif*.

Mann often compared the structure of his novels to musical structures and when he was satisfied with a book he called it a 'good score'. His use of *leitmotifs*—which is most prominent in *Doctor Faustus* but occurs in works as early as *Buddenbrooks*—was influenced by Wagner, and his juxtaposition of themes has the complexity and intellectual rigour of the juxtaposition of musical themes. The comparison of the structure of a novel to that of a score, however, can be made only in highly metaphorical terms. Musical form, generally, is a question of purely musical principles. The *leitmotif* can be used as a literary device, but Mann's use of it is not like Wagner's. Mann's use is far more rigid than Wagner's, and whereas Wagner transforms and compounds motives to extend their meanings, Mann achieves Leverkühn's vivid portrait through (nearly) straightforward repetition. As a result, the character lacks the volatile power that the dæmonic must have if it is to reveal something more than a tortured human soul. Hagen's motives, for example, have the chilling melancholy attributed to Leverkühn, and his laugh is as cold as hell; his nightwatch, as he wishes Gunther and Siegfried joy on their journey, exhibits a combination of mockery and self-torture that characterises Leverkühn, too; but whereas Leverkühn attracts through the sympathy he commands (and this gives him a distinctly non-dæmonic aspect), Hagen's wickedness can burst forth with an irresistible geniality, blurring the distinctions between friendly and destructive exuberance (as in his call to his vassals), and thus the dæmonic character overwhelms by the way he persuades one, not to sympathise with him, but to participate in his disturbing exuberance. Mann's adoration of Nietzsche, which is sometimes tediously reflected by the narrator's love for Leverkühn, results in a character for whom one can feel affection and admiration alongside a somewhat uncomfortable awareness of ruthlessness and hostility; but Mann does not create a true dæmon.

Indeed, much of Mann's presentation of the dæmonic seems forced. When Zeitblom discovers Adrian at the piano of his uncle's house exploring, with a flushed face which reveals unusual excitement, the ambiguities of the key system and the way enharmonics can be used as modulation, the narrator says he felt amazed and even ashamed at his discovery of a passion of Adrian's. Relationship is everything, Adrian explains to his startled friend; and this remark is supposed to be connected to the breakdown of the old morality that had depended upon the belief in absolute values. 'Relationship is everything' is used to make the implication that 'everything is ambiguous'; but the former does not imply the latter. 'Relationship is everything' might mean that something (a chord, a moral value?) has a determinate form only within a given context, or that what it is, is clear only when the context is known; it does not mean that a chord (or the value of something?) is never determinate and always ambiguous. Moreover, Zeitblom's anxiety about Adrian's discovery overlooks the fact that such key ambiguity was widely used by composers of the classical style; the brightest, healthiest of all composers—Haydn—was a master of enharmonic modulation. It is, then, not at all clear why such harmonic ambiguity should be thought to indicate anything dæmonic in Adrian's musical interests.

The dæmonic elements in nature, too, are presented with unsatisfactory contrivance. Adrian's father, who represents the fine, old German type, with his honest simplicity and earnest, catholic interests, feels reverence for the oddities of nature, but Zeitblom believes—and his belief is endorsed by the obvious similarity of Jonathan Leverkühn's naturalistic studies to those described in the Faust chapbook—there is something of witchcraft or forbidden magic in the attempt to tease nature into revealing her various techniques: 'Nature itself is too full of obscure phenomena not altogether remote from magic—equivocal moods, weird, half-hidden associations pointing to the unknown—for the disciplined piety not to see therein a rash over-stepping of ordained limits'.[6] The weirdness of various natural phenomena is asserted without qualification or explanation, as though scientific curiosity itself were irreverent. Mann connects this weirdness-of-nature motive to Adrian's pact with the devil, for Adrian calls the prostitute who infects him (and his syphilis represents his pact with the devil, for it is the means whereby he believes he will heighten his powers, but deny the possibility of a good, human life) 'Haetera Esmeralda', which is the name of the clear-winged butterflies Jonathan Leverkühn studied.

This name also provides the basis for the note-row of Leverkühn's first serial composition—his first composition, that is, in the style that provides a language for modern, dæmonic reality. The *leitmotif* and its associated themes are tools for insistence rather than a development of the dæmonic image.

The medieval atmosphere is more convincingly achieved. Germany itself is shown to be an essentially backward-looking nation, and the apparently modernistic ruthlessness is shown to be a hearkening back to a medieval consciousness. The substantial criticisms Mann makes of this Gothic-Romanticism pertain to the sadism-based morality and the dæmonic-based religion which underlies it. Leverkühn begins his university studies at Halle, where he belongs to the theology department. One of his teachers—Kumpf—is a parody of Luther, or, rather, of Luther's vulgar simplicity. Kumpf's hatred of the devil is so personal and immediate that it conjures up the devil and makes him a constant companion. Luther threw an inkwell at the devil, and Kumpf throws rolls; the imagination that makes the devil so vivid reveals an imagination that needs the sadistic thrill of the dæmonic image. Leverkühn's other teacher, Schleppfuss, openly acknowledges his affinity, as a man of God, with the devil. Goodness is meaningless, he argues, without the possibility of evil, and good can therefore be understood and appreciated only when evil is understood and appreciated. Like Naphta, the theology professor believes that people crave the cruelty that goes hand in hand with this view of the spiritual struggling up from the dæmonic swamp; he claims that the victims of the Inquisition were actually grateful for their punishments, because such punishments purged them from the evil which they genuinely attributed to themselves. The Inquisition thrived upon the victims' need for such judgements, Schleppfuss insists; and, in modern terms, this is reflected in the National Socialists' view that pain is a purge, a refreshment of the spirit and culture, and that Germany wants to suffer the torture that will give her new life. But the medieval devil does not provide a satisfactory image for the modern dæmonic. When Leverkühn himself adopts a medieval tone and a medieval religious manner, as he does in writing to Zeitblom about the guide who brought him to the Leipzig brothel (the guide reminds him of Schleppfuss and, being lame, he bears the mark of his twin's name), he adopts the tone to mock it; yet, at the same time, the dæmonic-religious atmosphere is unquestionably real, and the mockery is a disguise for his confusion and moral fear. Leverkühn must realise the image of the modern devil; his confusion and fear must become more self-aware and less superstitious; and, thus, he turns from theology to music.

Leverkühn as composer has an affinity with the dæmonic partly through his affinity with music, whose sensuous domination threatens the spirit (though in Leverkühn's works, with their severe intellectual structure, this aspect is not dominant) and whose access to the primitive, destructive—creative will threatens normal life and morality. More specific to his impasse as a contemporary composer is his need to develop a language capable of giving expression to the modern state of man and his world. This modern state consists of chaos, licence and savagery; here the dark, unreflecting forces of life are glorified in their cruellest aspects. The power to express such spiritual deprivation, the capacity to give form to moral chaos and emotional licence, can be provided only by the devil's language, for these states belong to the devil. Thus Leverkühn makes his pact. But what if the use of the devil's language, the exposure of the devil's estate, were to result in horror of evil rather than in celebration? What if, through spiritual deprivation, one discovered an undeniable longing for spirit and a recognition of the necessity of morality? Could not the use of the devil's language be a sacrifice of one's moral and spiritual impulses for the purpose of discovering their ultimate reality, and thus, could not the sacrifice point towards redemption? This is the essentially unanswered question that surrounds Leverkühn's creative endeavours.

The image of the artist as someone who sacrifices himself to his art is not new in Mann's work, but *Doctor Faustus* does present a new conception of the nature of that sacrifice. Tonio Kröger envied the people whose lives he described in his books; he, as an artist, as the discoverer of inward laws and truths, was denied active life. Aschenbach was destroyed as he tried to overstep the boundaries his art drew around his life; as an artist he could not handle the upsurge of immediate life. But *Doctor Faustus*, carrying on from *Mario and the Magician*, in which Cipolla claims to suffer the pain he persuades others to express, presents the artist as someone who bears the burden of life more intensely than the ordinary man. The artist is still not an active participant in life (when the artist steps into life he becomes a pathetic and dangerous figure: Hitler had wanted to be a great architect, and referred to himself as a frustrated artist) but he is nonetheless bound especially close to the forces underlying life. His individuality, his personal emotions and history, are sacrificed to his ability to express the collective psyche. In *Buddenbrooks* and *Tonio Kröger* 'life' was simple, unreflecting activity and immediate, practical desire; it was sometimes banal and sometimes rather fetching, but it was always innocuous. In *Doctor Faustus* the unreflecting activity is the artist's subject, yet it is anything but innocuous. Hanno's death drift has become aggressive; it is active, and therefore destructive; the practical world and the artist's world are one, and the mingling is the devil's achievement.

The artist, in this novel too, is still separated from the world of human attachment and affection, and this theme is still portrayed with a good deal of sentimentality. Leverkühn's nephew, who dies from meningitis and whose death Leverkühn sees as his own responsibility (because he loved him in spite of his dæmonic pact) is too sweet and benevolent and innocent to be convincing. Moreover, the connection between Leverkühn's behaviour and the child's illness is too arbitrary to provide any justification for his sense of guilt. The themes of this novel do indeed point to the need to reassess responsibility for disasters one did not foresee or intend; but to make any sense of responsibility some kind of causal link must be argued. Leverkühn's pact with the devil is real because the devil's world is real and because the composer's imagination, with almost exultant determination, explored that world; but the devil does not have the reality of Kumpf's devil, at whom one could throw rolls, nor the reality of an overseer who, like Faust's Mephistopheles, becomes a personal agent in the drama. More convincing—because given an explanation in terms of human motive and desire—is Leverkühn's unwitting instigation of tragedy when he sends Schwertfeger to propose on his behalf to Marie Godeau. Schwertfeger understands his errand to be a travesty, yet he, the flirtatious violinist, is sycophant to the composer. He goes, but the confrontation ends with him suing for Marie Godeau's hand himself, and, as a result of his engagement, his mistress shoots him. Here the artist's emotional awkwardness is seen on a human plane; his coldness is not presented as a privileged quality, but as part of the world's confusion and ignorance.

In *Doctor Faustus* the artist still suffers in isolation, as did Tonio Kröger, but his suffering is no longer narcissistic and self-indulgent. Leverkühn's isolation intensifies the universal element of his art; for in isolation from specific conflicts and desires, he faces the bare bones of the moral problem: he goes to the farthest extreme of evil to warn against that path or to find a way through it. Furthermore, the chilling aspect of Leverkühn's solitary journey makes, dramatically, an important moral point. As Leverkühn explains the meaning of his final composition to his friends (who are all, in various ways, representative of Germany and who, therefore, are ultimately the subjects of his work), they either recoil from him or mock his agony or declare him, when he is revealing their own reality, to be mad. Leverkühn strikes a dissonant chord on the piano and then opens his mouth as though to sing; but instead he utters a horrible, heart-piercing cry. When he collapses even the faithful Zeitblom hesitates to approach him. Only Frau Schweigestill, whose wholesome humanity has remained inviolate, despite the moral decay around her, is free from the egoism which fears contact with illness and injury; only her healthy understanding makes her care effective, and prevents any gap between the perception of suffering and sympathetic action.

This episode reveals a continuing force against evil in traditional humanism—humanism which is importantly different from the shallow, feeble enlightenment of the burgher classes, which the proud Faust, in Leverkühn's final composition, totally rejects. Whereas 'enlightened' society, with its hypocritical restraints, destroys people like the Rodde sisters, Frau Schweigestill offers her lodgers reprieve from the false urban morality. She describes a schizophrenic who had once stayed with her as a woman whose ideas had not been able to fit in with those of the rest of the world: Frau Schweigestill is too sensitive to suffering to be intolerant of madness. She also cared for a pregnant Fraülein, and she sees the young woman's parents' despair as both ridiculous and cruel because it is brought on by finicky social fears and prevents them from giving their daughter the love she needs. Frau Schweigestill does not deny the darker side of human nature because she is not shocked by it. Nor does she dwell upon sin with the fascination of the guilty. The key to her sanity and morality is effective, immediate sympathy.

Towards the end of his life, when he is paralysed as a result of syphilis, Leverkühn has—according to Zeitblom—a Christ-like appearance. Though this association is somewhat simplistic, the novel as a whole supports the conception of the artist as a man who, like no other, explores and suffers the extreme depths of the soul and the psyche. In the grip of passion and pain the artist discovers his ultimate humanity and his ultimate morality. The model is a Romantic one, for gigantic, uncompromising forces are seen as the greatest reality, and the hero is the one who exhausts himself in his struggle with these forces, who is destroyed and redeemed through his destruction. For the Flying Dutchman, caught within the sea's tumultuous yearning and strife, to be drowned is to be freed; and the impetus of this novel is towards spiritual redemption through immersion in the will.

As Romanticism's prime representative, music provides the dramatic focus of the novel. It is music that combines the best and worst impulses: it is music that discovers the devil's language in its supreme suitability for the expression of the chaotic and savage will, and it is also music, which arose from lamentation, that will reveal an irreducible spiritual craving. Leverkühn's world is a musical one; but the artistic bias of his life does not limit him (as it limited Tonio Kröger and Aschenbach). The musical world penetrates the human world and extends it to reveal its deepest sources.

Frau Leverkühn's melodious mezzo-soprano speaking voice, with its instinctive sweetness and warmth, was, from the hour of Adrian's birth, his lullaby. As a child Adrian learned counterpoint from Hanne, the stable girl, who, smelling of her good and useful animals, sang part-songs with him and Zeitblom in the evenings under the linden tree. The songs she sang were often gruesome and mawkish, and her simplicity introduces a sinister element in Adrian's musical world. The folk-songs reveal a taste for cruelty. Their medieval flavour is reflected in the medieval setting of Leverkühn's first disciplined musical instruction—the city of Kaisersaschern—where Adrian is taught by a man who left America because it was too progressive and who clings to the backward-looking conservatism that thrives in the heart of Germany. Despite Kretzschmar's view of music as the human spirit's finest and most subtle spokesman, it is he who introduces Adrian to the notion that the classical style is at an end. His description of the consummation of the classical style, however, is hardly pessimistic, for it employs a thoroughly positive conception of music as an art that involves one's sensuous and emotional being but at the same time provides a language for the spirit. As Kretzschmar, battling against his stutter, discusses the question as to why Beethoven did not write a third movement to his last piano sonata (opus 111), he plays the second and final variations movement:

> The arietta theme, destined to vicissitudes for which in it idyllic innocence it would not seem to have been born, is presented at once, and announced in sixteen bars, reducible to a motif which appears at the end of its first half, like a brief soul-cry . . . What happens now to this mild utterance, to this pensive, subdued

formulation rhythmically, harmonically, contrapuntally, with what does its master bless and to what condemns it, into what black nights and dazzling flashes, crystal spheres wherein coldness and heat, repose and ecstasy are one and the same, he flings it down and lifts it up . . .

The characteristic of the movement is of course the wide gap between bass and treble, between the right and left hand, and a moment comes, an utterly extreme situation, when the delicate motif seems to hover alone and forsaken above a giddy yawning abyss—a procedure of awe-inspiring unearthliness, from which then succeeds a distressful diminishing, something like a start of fear that such a thing could happen. Much else happens before the end. But when it ends, and while it is ending, something arrives, after so much rage, persistence, obstinacy, extravagance: something entirely unexpected and touching in its mildness and goodness. With the motif passed through many vicissitudes, which takes leave and in so doing becomes itself an entire farewell, a parting wave and call, with this DGG occurs a slight change, it undergoes a small melodic expansion. After an introductory C, it puts a C-sharp before D, [. . .] and this added C-sharp is the most moving, consolatory, pathetically reconciling thing in the world. It is like having one's hair stroked, lovingly, understandingly, like a deep and silent farewell look. It blesses the object, the desperately harried formulation, with overpowering humanity, it lies in parting so gently on the hearer's heart in eternal farewell that the eyes run over [. . .] Then it breaks off. Quick, hard triplets hasten to a conclusion with which any other piece might have ended.

[. . .] We only had needed, [Kretzschmar] said, to hear the piece to answer the question. A third movement? A new approach—after this farewell? A return—after this separation? Impossible! It had happened that the sonata had come, in the second, enormous movement, to an end, an end without any return.

Chapter 8, pp. 56–7

Despite the vicissitudes to which music itself is shown to be subject in this novel, Kretzschmar's type of musical analysis remains valid. Music expresses man's battle with spiritual and dæmonic forces, and on the musical battlefield the composer seeks his ultimate, heroic resolution in tenderness and lamentation. The Romanticism of

Wagner, which Mann saw as a burden of longing, a passive dissolution of the senses and spirit which drifts towards death, has been replaced by the Romantic heroism of Beethoven and Nietzsche, in which resolution is triumph and exultation, and death is a lamenting departure rather than an ecstatic greeting.

In many respects Leverkühn's struggles have a moral clarity those of Hans Castorp and Aschenbach lack. Leverkühn's discovery of hope is through the despair of hell, and Mann shows how the good aspects of the German character and the good aspects of Romanticism have been distorted into the greatest evil; but there is not, in this novel, the moral ambiguity of *The Magic Mountain* in which the most desirable is the most deadly, or of *Death in Venice* in which the abyss provides imagination's richest promise and yet is totally destructive. In *Doctor Faustus* Mann's hell (which is a place in which evil is celebrated rather than a place in which evil is punished) is moral annihilation, and the underworld is not the seductive-dæmonic or fascinating wildness or release from shallow practicality; savagery and licence are deprived of their aura of lush vitality, and hell breeds them in awful isolation. The devil tells Adrian:

> That is the secret delight and security of hell, that it is not to be informed upon, that is is protected from speech, that it just is, but cannot be public in the newspapers, be brought by any word to critical knowledge, wherefore precisely the words 'subterranean', 'cellar', 'thick walls', 'soundlessness', 'forgottenness', hopelessness', are poor weak symbols. One must be satisfied by symbolism, my good man, when one is speaking of hell, for there everything ends—not only the true word that describes, but everything altogether . . . Every compassion, every grace, every sparing every last trace of consideration for the incredulous, imploring objection 'that verily you cannot do so unto a soul': it is done, it happens, and indeed without being called to any reckoning in words; in a soundless cellar, far down beneath God's hearing, and happens to all eternity.

> Chapter 25, p. 238

The horror rather than the fascination of hell is emphasised in *Doctor Faustus*. The devil explains that what are normally referred to as the 'lusts of hell' is excitation from continuous pain, an excitation which destroys the dignity of suffering. Everyone is in pain, yet everyone mocks his neighbour for his pain. Suffering here, in the devil's hell, leads not to compassion but to sadism and jeering. Adrian uses this image of hell in his music, for it is this—this counterpart to Germany's soul—which he must express; but in this hell Adrian discovers his humanity and music discovers its proper subject as lamentation, and the devil's hell is, possibly, redeemed.

Mann's account of the development of musical form is strongly influenced by his moral vision and lacks historical incisiveness. Kretzschmar's view that the second movement of opus 111 is the consummation and thus the end of sonata form, is based upon the expressive rather than the harmonic or structural aspects of the music: the movement is seen as a leavetaking after which there can be no return. But of course there was a return to this form, though the classical style itself had come to an end. Leverkühn's creative impasse, during the period in which he could write only parodistic works, seems to imply that between Beethoven and possible contemporary styles there was a huge gap; whereas Schumann, Brahms and Debussy (and of course Wagner) formed a bridge without which contemporary music as it is, is unimaginable. Moreover, the devil's explanation as to why the composer needs his dæmonic gifts makes little sense as a musical argument. He tells Adrian that the devil's function is not to destroy value through reductive criticism (as did Goethe's Mephistopheles) but to rule with 'shining, sparkling, vainglorious unreflectingness'. This amoral, instinctive energy must be Adrian's subject matter and, the devil argues, to realise this subject the composer needs a strict and dæmonic style. Again his argument is moral rather than musical: a musical style given by God would allow freedom, as God allows freedom, but the devil is a despot; secondly, godly forms appeal to the understanding, whereas the barbaric and elemental subject matter the devil provides, confounds and terrorises the understanding.

The sometimes simplistic, sometimes contrived account of Leverkühn's musical form is mitigated by Mann's masterly descriptions of the compositions themselves. In these descriptions the musical forms chosen by Leverkühn are indeed shown to be necessary to musical expression. *Apocalypsis cum figuris*, Adrian's penultimate oratorio uses the devil's language to reveal a highly disturbing paradox; for in this composition, dissonance is used to express everything lofty, solemn, pious, everything of the spirit, whereas the consonance of classical harmony is reserved for the world of hell. The paradox arises from the fact that the world is now in harmony with hell, and the 'rightness' associated with classical tonality, the sense of its belonging to an objective order, stems from its correspondence with the true nature of the world, which is now the devil's nature.

The awfulness, and the greatness, of this work are frighteningly clear. At the end of the first part of the oratorio there is a hellish laughter which represents the devil's hell: 'for this bliss of hell is like a deep-voiced pitiful jeering and scorn of all the immeasurable anguish'.[7] In the musical work the laughter begins with a single voice and then rapidly gains ground, embracing choir and orchestra, until it explodes in the mocking, exulting laughter of the Pit. Yet this hellish laughter has its counterpart in the beginning of the second part of the oratorio, where a children's choir is accompanied by a chamber orchestra to achieve an icy, cosmic effect, with harsh dissonances, but also with an apparent effect of inaccessible, supernatural and alien loveliness of sound that fills the hearer with a hopeless longing. The spiritual impasse is clear when one understands that this music of the spheres reproduces, note for note, the music of hell's mocking laughter. The devil has usurped heaven, and the longing, which Zeitblom says is felt within the work, the longing for a soul, is a longing without hope.

When Leverkühn discusses the terms of his pact with the devil he proposes the possibility that contrition will eventually save him. The devil answers that contrition for the sake of salvation is worthless. Leverkühn insists he means genuine contrition which is too profound to consider the possibility of salvation: what then? The devil evades Leverkühn's question, and the question re-emerges with Leverkühn's final work, *D. Fausti Weheklag* which, ultimately, defeats the devil. The most profoundly dæmonic aspect of the earlier oratorio was the fact that hell's barbarism gave rise to mockery, that universal suffering was divorced from compassion, that there was absolutely no viable moral position in that ecstasy of chaos and impulse. The initial conception of his final work is equally savage and negative: after the death of his nephew, Leverkühn declares his determination to 'take back' Beethoven's Ninth Symphony. He plans to deny the vision of universal love, joy and communion with which Beethoven's work concludes. But this denial is not a negation of religion; its denial is couched in terms of lamentation, which reveal reverence for the lost vision. Moreover, in this work Leverkühn rediscovers music's first and original manifestation as lamentation; and lamentation is expression, and expression is liberation. The work has a highly determined structure, but the expressive element supersedes this rigour; finally, the cellar walls of hell are broken, and music gives a hearing to man's spiritual needs and offers a recognition of his humanity.

This enormous work is, like the finale of the Ninth Symphony with its variations of exultation, a variation-piece, but it is negatively related to Beethoven's work in that the variations are a series of laments, and there is no spiritual expansion, but always a return to the theme, based upon Faust's saying in the sixteenth-century chapbook, 'For I die as a good and bad Christian'. His goodness stems from his contrition; his badness from his pact with the devil; but Leverkühn changes the notion of a Christian as someone who might be saved. Indeed, the very hope of salvation is the devil's temptation, and, in proud despair, Faust says 'No' to the false and feeble burgher's God.

There is no going back to the traditional religion in which it is supposed that reason and goodwill triumph. In this respect Leverkühn is dæmonic, for he, like Nietzsche, prefers the devil's truth to comforting falsehood. Yet the very strength of his despair and his proud commitment to truth and the genuine assessment of human suffering is a gesture towards redemption:

at the end of this work of ceaseless lamentation, softly, above reason, and with the speaking unspokenness given to music alone, it touches the feelings. I mean the closing movement of the piece, where the choir loses itself and which sounds like the lament of God over the lost state of His world . . . This dark tone-poem permits up to the very end no consolation, appeasement, transfiguration. But take our artistic paradox: grant that expressiveness— expressiveness as lament—is the issue of the whole construction. Then may we not set it parellel to another conception, a religious one, and ask, but only in the lowest whisper, whether out of the thoroughly irremediable hope might germinate? It would be a hope beyond hopelessness, the transcendence of despair—not a betrayal of it, but the miracle, which goes beyond belief. Listen to the end alone, listen with me. One group of instruments after another retires, and what remains, as the work fades in the air, is the high G of a cello, the last word, the last fainting sound, slowly dying in a pianissimo-fermata. Then nothing more—silence and night. But that tone which vibrates in the silence, which is no more, upon which only the spirit meditates, and which was the voice of mourning, is so no more, it changes its meaning, it remains like a light in the night.

Chapter 46, p. 471

Schopenhauer believed that man discovered a compassion-based morality when he realised the universality of the chaotic forces that lie behind life and death. The horror of the devil's hell is the ignominious thrill of pain and the continuous desire to wound and to mock one's companions in pain. Leverkühn, as he uses the devil's language and presents the devil's world, develops his own human voice—the voice of lamentation—and this is a discovery of his own humanity, of his participation in all suffering and of the necessity of a new morality. It is a morality based on a thoroughly pessimistic view of the world, as was Schopenhauer's, but it is also the only morality that seemed honest at the time of the composition.

Leverkühn worked on *D. Fausti Weheklag* during the last two years of his rational existence (1929–30), years which bred the disasters that overwhelmed the country, disasters which, as Zeitblom finishes his biography (in the last phase of the Second World War), are being drowned in blood and flame. Adrian dies in 1940, just when, as Zeitblom puts it, Germany, at the height of her corrupt triumphs, was about to gain the whole world by her pact with the devil. And now the country 'embraced by demons, a hand over one eye and with the other staring into horrors, falls down from abyss to abyss. When from the uttermost hopelessness will a miracle, which goes beyond belief, light the day of hope?'[8]

Germany, trying to seek national identity through a political glorification of the Romanticism that was part of the country's art, has discovered herself to be at the mercy of her self-created dæmons. Zeitblom's prayer for his country, which closes the novel, echoes the close of Leverkühn's last work: when the will has its way, when reason and morality are thoroughly overpowered, then man draws his breath and looks at his evil world and rediscovers his need for reason and restraint. But there is no going back to a belief in the possibility of man as a rational being, whose deepest desires and interests lead to goodness and harmony. The irrational, the aggressive and the destructive have been revealed as the largest part of human nature; yet the horror of this revelation is such that some moderation of man's dæmonic reality is seen to be necessary—absolutely necessary.

The moral tale is darker than that of *The Magic Mountain*, with its similar ending, when it is proposed that love might arise from the world-feast of death and destruction. Here the hope is meagre, but for the Romanticist it is a triumph. *Doctor Faustus* exhibits a felt need for a restraining morality in a way that transcends a Romanticist's view—a view in which death and dissolution and the power of passion and impulse are seen as the highest goods. Yet the drama in which this frail but essential moral standpoint is secured, is itself highly Romantic. The notion of redemption from the uttermost point of despair, of building up only from destruction, of finding truth only through forbidden journeys, reveals an abiding sympathy with Romantic extremity and intensity and with the peculiar life-defeat that accompanies them, a life-defeat based upon an enormous vitality that cannot integrate itself with reality. *Doctor Faustus* is a triumph for Mann's imagination in that the necessity of morality is discovered in the depth of a Romanticist's tale, but even this triumph is conceived only as the final, despairing, Romantic gesture.

References

All references to German works are to standard English translations. I have modified the translations in my text when I found them too free or not in keeping with the style of the original German.

1 Introduction
1. F. Nietzsche, *Beyond Good and Evil*, trans. W. Kaufmann (New York: Vintage Books, 1966), Part 1, sec. 13.
2. F. Nietzsche, *On the Genealogy of Morals*, trans. W. Kaufmann (New York: Vintage Books, 1969), Second Essay, sec. 22. p. 93.
3. T. Mann, 'Freud and the Future', in *Thomas Mann Essays*, trans. H. T. Lowe-Porter (New York: Vintage Books, 1957).
4. T. Mann, 'Goethe, Novelist', in *Past Masters and Other Papers*, trans. H. T. Lowe-Porter (London: Martin Secker, 1933), p. 110.
5. *Beyond Good and Evil*, op. cit., Part 4, sec. 171.

2 The Romantic Dilemma
1. T. Mann, *Buddenbrooks*, trans. H. T. Lowe-Porter (Middlesex: Penguin, 1957). All references to *Buddenbrooks* are to this edition.
2. Ibid, part 3, chapter 9, p. 115.
3. Ibid, part 2, chapter 2, p. 56.
4. H. James, 'The Lesson of the Master', in *Selected Short Stories* (Middlesex, Penguin, 1963), p. 82.
5. T. Mann, *Death in Venice, Tristan, Tonio Kröger*, trans. H. T. Lowe-Porter (Middlesex, Penguin, 1962). All references to these stories are to this edition.
6. T. Mann, *Royal Highness*, trans. A. Cecil Curtis, revised by C. McNab (Middlesex: Penguin, 1975), p. 9. All references to *Royal Highness* are to this edition.

3 The Death Enchantment
1. T. Mann, 'Sufferings and Greatness of Richard Wagner', in *Thomas Mann Essays*, op. cit., p. 206.
2. T. Mann, *Tristan*, op. cit., p. 112.
3. T. Mann, 'Sleep, Sweet Sleep', in *Past Masters and Other Papers*, op. cit.
4. Ibid., p. 278.
5. For a detailed discussion of Wagner's *Ring* as a psychic drama see R. Donnington, *Wagner's 'Ring' and its Symbols*, 3rd edition (London: Faber and Faber, 1974).
6. T. Mann, *Little Herr Friedemann and Other Stories*, trans. H. T. Lowe-Porter (Middlesex: Penguin, 1972), p. 116.

7. Ibid., p. 184.
8. Ibid., p. 179.
9. T. Mann, *Death in Venice*, op. cit., pp. 9–10.
10. Ibid., p. 59.
11. Ibid., p. 61.
12. Ibid., p. 73.
13. Ibid., p. 71.
14. Ibid., p. 83.

4 *The Fascination of Disgust*
1. T. Mann, *The Magic Mountain*, trans. H. T. Lowe-Porter (Middlesex: Penguin, 1962). All references to *The Magic Mountain* are to this edition.
2. Ibid., chapter 5, p. 229.
3. Ibid., chapter 6, p. 478.
4. *Death in Venice*, op. cit., p. 55.
5. Ibid., pp. 55–6.
6. Ibid., chapter 5, p. 227.
7. *the Magic Mountain*, op. cit., chapter 7, p. 652.
8. Ibid, chapter 7, p. 653.

5 *Mann and Lawrence*
1. D. H. Lawrence, *Women in Love* (Middlesex: Penguin, 1968). All references to *Women in Love* are to this edition.
2. Ibid, 'Sisters', p. 24.
3. D. H. Lawrence, 'Thomas Mann', in *Selections from Phoenix*, ed. A. A. M. Inglis (Middlesex: Penguin, 1971), p. 282.
4. *Women in Love*, op. cit., 'Sisters', p. 8.
5. Ibid. 'The Industrial Magnate', p. 244.
6. *The Magic Mountain*, op. cit., chapter 5, p. 313.

6 *Myth and Resolution*
1. M. Eliade, *Myths, Dreams and Reveries*, trans. P. Mairet (London: Collins, 1974), p. 23.
2. T. Mann, *Joseph and His Brothers*, trans. H. T. Lowe-Porter (London: Sphere Books, 1968). All references to this work are to the four volumes of this edition.
3. Ibid., *Tales of Jacob*, p. 160.
4. Ibid., *Joseph in Egypt*, p. 283.

7 *Mann and Goethe*
1. 'Goethe, Novelist', in *Past Masters and Other Papers*, op. cit.
2. J. P. Eckermann, *Conversations with Goethe*, trans. J. Oxenford (London: Everyman Library, 1971), p. 181.
3. Ibid., p. 8.
4. T. Mann, *Lotte in Weimar*, trans. H. T. Lowe-Porter (Middlesex: Penguin, 1968), p. 305. All reference to *Lotte in Weimar* are to this edition.

8 *The Nihilistic Face of Aestheticism*
1. *Thomas Mann Essays*, op. cit., p. 226.
2. T. Mann, *Confessions of Felix Krull, Confidence Man*, trans. D. Lindley

(Middlesex: Penguin, 1965). All references to *Felix Krull* are to this edition.
3. F. Nietzsche, *Gay Science*, from *The Portable Nietzsche*, ed. and trans. W. Kaufmann (London: Chatto and Windus, 1971), p. 683.
4. *Felix Krull*, op. cit., Part One, chapter 2, p. 15.
5. Ibid., Part 1, chapter 3, p. 17.
6. Ibid., Part 3, chapter 4, p. 212.
7. Ibid., Part 1, chapter 5, p. 25.
8. Ibid., p. 25.
9. Ibid., Part 3, chapter 11, p. 347.

9 Dæmonic Redemption
1. A. Speer, *Inside the Third Reich*, trans. R. and C. Winston (London: Sphere Books, 1971), pp. 46–7.
2. 'Nietzsche and Music', in *Past Master and Other Papers*, op. cit., p. 43.
3. 'Cosmopolitanism' in *Past Master and Other Papers*.
4. T. Mann, *Doctor Faustus*, trans. H. T. Lowe-Porter (Middlesex: Penguin, 1968), chapter 2, p. 13. All references to *Doctor Faustus* are to this edition.
5. 'Nietzsche and Music', in *Past Masters and Other Papers*, op. cit.
6. *Doctor Faustus*, op. cit., chapter 3, p. 18.
7. Ibid., chapter 25, p. 239.
8. Ibid, Epilogue, p. 490.

Bibliography of the Principal Works of Thomas Mann

First Editions in English. Translated, where not otherwise stated, by H. T. Lowe-Porter and now published in London by Martin Secker & Warburg and in New York by Alfred A. Knopf. For other editions actually cited in the text, please see the References.

Royal Highness: A Novel of German Court Life, translated by A. Cecil Curtis (Sidgwick & Jackson, 1916)
In the translation of H. T. Lowe-Porter with a foreword by the author (Martin Secker & Warburg, 1940)
Bashan and I, translated by Herman George Scheffauer (Collins, 1923). As *A Man and His Dog* included in *Stories of Three Decades* (*vide*) translated by H. T. Lowe-Porter
Buddenbrooks, 2 vols (Martin Secker, 1924); 1 vol (Martin Secker, 1930); new edn (1962)
Death in Venice, translated by Kenneth Burke, and published in New York 1925. Contains the title-story, *Tristan*, and *Tonio Kröger* (Martin Secker, 1928)
The Magic Mountain, 2 vols (Martin Secker, 1927); 1 vol (Martin Secker, 1928); new edn (1961)
Children and Fools, translated by Herman George Scheffauer. Nine stories, including translations of 'Der kleine Herr Friedemann' and 'Unordnung und frühes Leid (not published in England) (New York, 1928)
A Sketch of My Life (Harrison of Paris, 1930)
Three Essays, contains translations of 'Friedrich und die grosse Koalition' from 'Rede und Antwort,' and of 'Goethe und Tolstoi' and 'Okkulte Erlebnisse' from 'Bemühungen' (Martin Secker, 1932)
Early Sorrow, a story (Martin Secker, 1929)
Mario and the Magician (Martin Secker, 1930)

Past Masters and Other Papers (Martin Secker, 1933)

Joseph and His Brethren, I. The Tales of Jacob (Martin Secker, 1934);
II. Young Joseph (Martin Secker, 1935); III. Joseph in Egypt, 2
vols (Martin Secker & Warburg, 1938); IV. Joseph the Provider
(Martin Secker & Warburg, 1945)

Stories of Three Decades, contains a preface by Thomas Mann and all
his fiction prior to 1940 except the long novels (1936)

An Exchange of Letters. 'Friends of Europe' Publications, No. 52. With
a foreword by J. B. Priestley (1951). Translated by Eric Sutton,
included in the *Coming Victory of Democracy (vide)*

Freud, Goethe, Wagner, translated by H. T. Lowe-Porter and Rita
Matthias-Reil. Three essays, published in New York (1937)

The Coming Victory of Democracy, translated by Agnes E. Meyer
(Martin Secker & Warburg, 1938)

This Peace (New York, 1938)

The Living Thoughts of Schopenhauer (Cassell, 1939)

This War, translated by Eric Sutton (Martin Secker & Warburg,
1940)

Stories and Episodes. A selection made by E. F. Bozman. Everyman's
Library (Dent, 1940)

Lotte in Weimar (Martin Secker & Warburg, 1940)

The Transposed Heads, the story of Sita (Martin Secker & Warburg,
1941)

Order of the Day, political essays and speeches of two decades.
Translated by H. T. Lowe-Porter, Agnes E. Meyer, and Eric
Sutton (Martin Secker & Warburg, 1942)

Listen, Germany! Twenty-five radio messages to the German people
over the BBC (New York, 1943)

The Tables of the Law. First published in *The Ten Commandments*
(Cassell, 1945); limited edition (Martin Secker & Warburg, 1947)

Essays of Three Decades, with portrait frontispiece (Martin Secker &
Warburg, 1947)

*Doctor Faustus: The Life of the German Composer Adrian Leverkühn as
Told by a Friend* (Martin Secker & Warburg, 1949)

The Holy Sinner (Martin Secker & Warburg, 1952)

Confessions of Felix Krull, Confidence Man, translated by Denver
Lindley (Martin Secker & Warburg, 1955, 1977)

Stories of a Lifetime, 2 vols (Martin Secker & Warburg, 1961, 1970)

Index

There is no entry for Thomas Mann in the index. References to Mann's works are entered by the standard English titles.